marie claire

fresh

acknowledgments

A heartfelt thank you to Kay Scarlett and Juliet Rogers for giving me this beautiful book, and to Jackie Frank for allowing me the opportunity to do it. Another big thank you to Marylouise Brammer and Lulu Grimes for all their tireless work and enthusiasm in bringing this project to fruition. Thanks also to Diana Hill, for her way with my words.

My studio team were a dream, yet again. To Ross Dobson, an even bigger hug is owed this time around. Thank you for all your hard work, great food, laughter and occasional tuneless singing. We are also indebted to Geoff Lung for once again allowing us to turn his studio into our second home. Thank you for your generosity and the never-dull lunchtime discussions. Thanks also to Emma and Gerry for the endless teas, coffees and assistance in the studio.

Once again this book would not have been possible without Petrina Tinslay. Thank you a million times over for your beautiful photographs, calm assurance, generous guidance and friendship.

Thanks also to Mum and Dad for always being there, to Cathy, Joanna and Ken for their endless smiles and to Warwick for his constant support and for ensuring that the laughter kept coming.

A book called *Fresh* needs great ingredients, so thank you to Justin, Hugh and Stephan at Murdoch Produce, and the Piromalli family from Patricks, for their yummy fruit and vegetables. Many thanks also to Orson & Blake, Empire Homewares and The Bay Tree for their wonderful homewares. A big thank you to Shelley and Mud Australia for their beautifully coloured bowls and another huge hug for David Edmonds and his sublimely simple ceramics.

Published by Murdoch Books®, a division of Murdoch Magazines Pty Ltd.

AUSTRALIA
Murdoch Books® Australia
GPO Box 1203
Sydney NSW 1045
Phone: (612) 4352 7000
Fax: (612) 4352 7026

UK
Murdoch Books UK Ltd
Ferry House, 51–57 Lacy Road
Putney, London SW15 1PR
Phone: + 44 (0) 20 8355 1480
Fax: + 44 (0) 20 8355 1499

Author and Stylist: Michele Cranston
Photographer: Petrina Tinslay
Creative Director: Marylouise Brammer
Food Director, Project Manager: Lulu Grimes
Food Preparation: Ross Dobson
Editor: Diana Hill

Chief Executive: Juliet Rogers
Publisher: Kay Scarlett
Production Manager: Kylie Kirkwood

National Library of Australia Cataloguing-in-Publication Data
Cranston, Michele. Fresh. Includes index.
ISBN 1 74045 195 3. 1. Cookery (Natural Foods). I. Tinslay, Petrina.
II. Title. III. Title: Marie Claire. 641.564

Text © Michele Cranston 2002. Photography © Petrina Tinslay 2002.
Design © Murdoch Books® 2002.
Printed by Toppan Printing Hong Kong Co. Ltd. PRINTED IN CHINA. First printed 2002.

The publisher would like to thank the following for their assistance with photography:
AEG Kitchen Appliances, Liebherr Refrigeration and Wine Cellars; Breville Holdings Pty Ltd.

Those at risk from the effects of salmonella food poisoning (including the elderly, pregnant women and children) should consult their GP with any concerns about eating raw eggs.

marie claire

fresh

michele cranston

photography by
petrina tinslay

MURDOCH
BOOKS

contents

This book could just as easily have been called 'market', because it is all about the awareness and enjoyment of freshly picked seasonal produce. But it is also very much about fresh food freshly cooked. Newly harvested, flavourful fruit and vegetables only need the addition of a few harmonious ingredients and a little seasoning to make great food. Using fresh produce is not only the simplest way to cook dinner for friends or family, it is also the most exciting. Simply head off to your local shops or growers market in search of inspiration: a lush display of salad greens here and some creamy farmhouse cheeses across the way are

simply fresh

the makings of an instant springtime starter, while rhubarb stalks piled high on a counter in ruby-red bundles will become bowlfuls of luscious, stewed sweetness topped with a dollop of cream. In the same way, the recipes in *fresh* are easy, they take little time, and they all highlight the essential flavours of the ingredients. Seasonal cooking means extracting maximum impact from produce appropriate to that time of the year — not only indulging in summer stone fruits and crisp spring greens, but also enjoying the hearty, earthy flavours of winter vegetables. Nature has already dictated the flavours that perfectly suit each season, so select your ingredients and enjoy the best that fresh has to offer.

spring

Spring is all about leafy greens and the refreshing crunch of salads after the warming, robust dishes of winter. This is the season when you can enjoy citrus flavours, new season lamb and young vegetables. Now you can also start thinking of freshly steamed beans, asparagus spears lightly drizzled with butter, emerald-green peas, bowls of bitter greens, grilled fish and, of course, an extravagance of herbs. Herbs should always be bought in large bunches and used with very little restraint — they are the colour and taste of spring, and with their fresh clean flavour and texture they will never disappoint. You can bring even the dullest meal to life with the addition of a squeeze of lemon or lime and lashings of leafy herbs. And with so much fresh produce available, spring is the time to keep the table settings simple and let the food make an impression.

asparagus

artichokes

avocados

beans

spinach

peas

watercress

bok choy

spring onions

mint

snow peas

chokos

strawberries

mandarins

oranges

pineapples

melons

papaya

good ideas

minted peas

There really is nothing nicer than the old classic, minted green peas. Add some fresh mint to the cooking water, reserving the nicer leaves to fold through the finished dish. When the peas are cooked, drain them and then stir in the mint leaves, olive oil and lots of freshly ground black pepper.

papaya

The perfect breakfast is as easy as fresh red papaya rubbed with lime juice and served with yoghurt and sliced banana or raspberries. If time is limited, blend the papaya with orange juice, banana and yoghurt for a delicious fruit whip.

asparagus

Freshly steamed asparagus needs little more than a drizzle of olive oil and lemon juice. However, there are other delicious options. Serve steamed asparagus 'soldiers' with a soft-boiled egg and crisp pancetta for a different take on an old breakfast favourite, or toss the spears with blanched beans and buttery spinach for a great warm side dish of greens.

bean salads

Green beans make a great base for a variety of flavourful salad combinations. Keep it simple with baby rocket (arugula) and a handful of parsley leaves, or try Chinese black beans, toasted almond slivers, chilli and lime juice. If you prefer lighter flavours, toss the beans with a little olive oil, orange juice, balsamic vinegar and fresh pistachio nuts.

lemons

Lemon juice always brings a light freshness to any dish, so it is ideal to add to any shop-bought sauces or pastes that need a bit of a lift. While lemons are in abundance, store some of the juice in frozen cubes ready for the leaner months and for those moments when you suddenly discover you need just a hint of citrus. If you love the taste of lemon in pastas, risottos and sauces, invest in a zester, which will remove the zest in fine, palatable strips.

marinated artichokes

It is no secret that fresh artichokes take time to prepare. If you always make a double batch you can enjoy a second serve on another occasion without any of the hard work. Marinate the artichokes in olive oil, lemon juice and fresh herbs and store them in the fridge until you are ready to enjoy them again in a few days' time.

capsicum salad with tuna and egg

poached tomato with goat's cheese

capsicum salad with tuna and egg

1 garlic clove, crushed

1 1/2 tablespoons red wine vinegar

3 tablespoons olive oil

1 green capsicum (pepper), finely diced

1 yellow capsicum (pepper), finely diced

3 ripe tomatoes, cut into wedges

150 g (3 handfuls) baby rocket (arugula) leaves

185 g (1/2 cup) tinned tuna, drained

4 hard-boiled eggs, quartered

30 g (1 cup) roughly chopped flat-leaf (Italian) parsley

Mix the garlic, vinegar, olive oil, diced capsicum and tomatoes together in a bowl. Pile four plates with baby rocket and top with the capsicum salad, tuna, boiled eggs and parsley. Season with salt and pepper. Serves 4

poached tomato with goat's cheese

4 large vine-ripened tomatoes

1 1/2 teaspoons sea salt

8 peppercorns

1 tablespoon balsamic vinegar

1/2 red onion, finely sliced

6 parsley sprigs

100 g (2 handfuls) rocket (arugula) leaves

4 tablespoons fresh pesto (basics)

115 g (4 oz) goat's cheese

Preheat the oven to 180°C (350°F/Gas 4). Put the tomatoes in a small, deep baking dish, then fill the dish with enough water to come halfway up the tomatoes. Add the sea salt, peppercorns, vinegar, onion and parsley stalks and bake for 40 minutes.

Divide the rocket between four plates. Lift the tomatoes out of the dish, arrange them on top of the rocket and drizzle each with some cooking liquid. Add some pesto and crumbled goat's cheese and serve. Serves 4

sardines on toast

3 ripe tomatoes, finely diced

1/2 red onion, finely sliced into rings

2 tablespoons white wine vinegar

2 tablespoons virgin olive oil

1 tablespoon oregano leaves

1 teaspoon butter

8 or 16 sardine fillets depending on their size
    (300 g/10 oz in total)

4 thick slices wholemeal bread, toasted

Put the tomatoes, onion, vinegar, olive oil and oregano leaves in a small bowl. Stir to combine and season with sea salt and freshly ground black pepper.

Put a nonstick pan over a high heat and add the butter. Fry the sardine fillets for 1 to 2 minutes on both sides until they are opaque and slightly browned, before piling them onto the toast. Top with the tomato salad and any remaining dressing. Serves 4

fresh and fast

• Serve a salad of rocket (arugula), crumbled blue cheese and fresh walnuts alongside seared lamb fillets.

• Put whole ripe Roma (plum) tomatoes on a baking tray. Bake them in a hot oven until the skin is blistered and blackened, then blend the whole tomatoes, including the charred skins, with a handful of fresh basil leaves and seasoning. Put the tomato mixture in a saucepan and add enough water or vegetable stock to form a soupy consistency. Heat the soup and serve with a drizzle of extra virgin olive oil and croutons.

• Add diced tomatoes and tinned white beans to tinned tuna. Lightly mash them together with a little olive oil and seasoning. Serve on bruschetta as a snack or with toasted rye bread as an easy lunch.

sardines on toast

potato salad

2 large Pontiac potatoes
6 spring onions (scallions), finely sliced
75 g (1/2 bunch) flat-leaf (Italian) parsley, roughly chopped
70 g (1 bunch) dill, finely chopped
125 ml (1/2 cup) olive oil
1 lemon, zested and juiced

Cut the potatoes into chunks, put them in a large saucepan of salted cold water and bring to the boil over a high heat. When the water has reached boiling point, cover the pan with a lid and remove it from the heat. Leave the potatoes to sit for half an hour. (This is a nice way to cook the potatoes because they don't break up or become waterlogged.)

Meanwhile, mix the spring onions, parsley, dill, olive oil, lemon juice and zest together. When the potatoes are ready, test them with the point of a sharp knife — they should be tender and cooked through. Drain them and add them to the herbed dressing while they are still hot. Toss to combine and season with salt and freshly ground black pepper. Serves 4

coconut prawns

4 egg whites
125 g (1 cup) plain (all-purpose) flour
100 g (1 2/3 cups) shredded or desiccated coconut
170 ml (2/3 cup) oil
20 raw prawns (shrimp), peeled and deveined
sweet chilli and ginger sauce
lime wedges

Whisk the egg whites until they are light and fluffy. Put the flour and coconut onto two separate plates. Heat a deep pan or wok and add the oil. While the oil is heating, toss one of the prawns in the flour, dip it into the egg white, and then roll it in the coconut. Set it aside. Repeat the process with the remaining prawns.

Once the oil has reached frying point (if you drop a coconut shred into the oil it will sizzle), carefully lower the prawns into the oil in batches of five. When the coconut has turned light brown on one side, turn the prawns over and cook until they are crisply golden on both sides. Remove the prawns and drain them on paper towels.

Serve with sweet chilli and ginger sauce and a squeeze of fresh lime. Makes 20

crab cocktail in a leaf

2 egg yolks
1 lemon, zested and juiced
250 ml (1 cup) light olive oil
1 teaspoon Dijon mustard
2 teaspoons finely chopped tarragon
1 tablespoon tomato paste (purée)
250 g (2 cups) fresh crab meat
16–20 baby gem lettuce leaves
Tabasco sauce

Whisk the egg yolks, lemon zest and juice together. Slowly drizzle in the oil, whisking the mixture until it becomes thick and creamy. Fold in the mustard, tarragon and tomato paste and set aside.

Break up the crab meat with a fork, leaving it in fairly large pieces, fold it into the dressing and season well. Spoon the crab into the baby gem leaves and top each with a dash of Tabasco. Makes 16 to 20

prawn sandwich

20 medium raw prawns (shrimp), peeled and deveined
60 ml (1/4 cup) lime juice
60 ml (1/4 cup) light olive oil
2 tablespoons oil
lime mayonnaise (basics)
8 slices white sourdough bread
coriander (cilantro) leaves

Put the prawns, lime juice and olive oil into a bowl and leave to marinate for half an hour.

Heat some of the oil in a heavy-based frying pan over a high heat. Put a few of the prawns into the pan and sear them for about 2 minutes, until they begin to curl. Flip them over and continue to cook them for a further minute until they are cooked through. Cook the rest of the prawns, a few at a time, in the same way.

Spread some lime mayonnaise onto each piece of bread. Divide the prawns between four slices, scatter with coriander leaves and season with white pepper. Top with the remaining bread. Serves 4

scallops with ginger and lemon grass

chicken and coconut soup

scallops with ginger and lemon grass

2 tablespoons finely chopped lemon grass
2 teaspoons grated fresh ginger
1/2 red chilli, seeded and finely chopped
1 tablespoon sesame oil
2 tablespoons mirin
1 tablespoon fish sauce
1 lime, juiced
12 scallops on the shell, cleaned
coriander (cilantro) leaves
lime wedges

Mix together the lemon grass, ginger, chilli, sesame oil, mirin, fish sauce and lime juice and leave to infuse for a few minutes.

Spoon a little of the marinade over each of the scallops and arrange them, still in their shells, in one or two steamer baskets. Put the steamer baskets over a saucepan of simmering water, cover and steam for 4 minutes, swapping the baskets after 2 minutes.

Remove the scallops from the baskets without letting any of the juices escape from the shells, and serve them with a sprinkle of coriander and lime wedges. Serves 2

chicken and coconut soup

1 teaspoon sesame oil
1 red chilli, seeded and finely sliced
2 chicken breast fillets, sliced thinly across the grain
4 spring onions (scallions), trimmed and sliced on the diagonal
1 red capsicum (pepper), finely sliced
1.5 litres (6 cups) chicken stock
1 x 400 ml (14 fl oz) tin coconut milk
3 tablespoons lime juice
1 tablespoon fish sauce
25 g (1/2 cup) chopped coriander (cilantro) leaves
100 g (4 handfuls) snow pea shoots, cut into short lengths
lime wedges

Put the sesame oil, chilli and chicken into a wok or saucepan over a moderate heat and stir-fry until the chicken is beginning to brown. Add the spring onions, capsicum, chicken stock, coconut milk, lime juice and fish sauce, bring to the boil and simmer for 10 minutes.

At the last minute, throw in the coriander and snow pea shoots. Season to taste with salt and pepper and serve immediately with lime wedges to squeeze over. Serves 4

three bean salad with prosciutto

6 slices prosciutto
175 g (6 oz) French beans
175 g (6 oz) wax beans
175 g (6 oz) tinned butter beans
2 tablespoons extra virgin olive oil
2 tablespoons white wine vinegar
30 g (1 cup) flat-leaf (Italian) parsley, roughly chopped
2 tablespoons toasted pine nuts

Put a large saucepan of water on to boil. Meanwhile, grill or pan-fry the prosciutto until it is crisp and then allow it to drain on a paper towel. Blanch the French and wax beans in the boiling water for a few minutes or until the green ones begin to turn an emerald green. Drain the beans and briefly refresh them under cold running water.

Return the beans to the saucepan with the butter beans and add the olive oil, vinegar and parsley. Break the prosciutto into small pieces and add it to the beans along with the pine nuts. Toss everything together and season with sea salt and black pepper. Pile onto a serving platter. Serves 4

fresh and fast

• Toss blanched green beans with olive oil and tapenade and serve with grilled tuna steaks.

• Tinned white beans are a great store cupboard stand-by. Combine them with fresh herbs and a little seasoning and serve alongside grilled lamb, or purée them with roasted garlic and olive oil and serve with pan-fried steak and grilled fresh tomatoes.

• Toss snow pea shoots in a quickly prepared dressing of lemon juice, olive oil, toasted sesame seeds and a little fresh ginger. Serve topped with grilled or barbecued fish.

three bean salad with prosciutto

Make an early spring morning visit to the local seafood markets and explore the endless array of fish and shellfish.

mussels with rouille

spring chowder

1.5 kg (3 lb 5 oz) cleaned clams
1 tablespoon light olive oil
1 garlic clove, crushed
2 streaky bacon rashers, chopped
2 white onions, diced
1 red chilli, seeded and finely chopped
1 carrot, grated
1 bay leaf
2 large desirée potatoes, peeled and diced
2 celery stalks, thinly sliced
30 g (1 cup) roughly chopped flat-leaf (Italian) parsley

Throw away any clams that don't close when you tap them. Bring 500 ml (2 cups) of water to the boil in a large saucepan, add the clams, then cover and cook for 2 to 3 minutes until they open. Discard any that stay closed. Take most of the clams out of their shells, keeping some whole for garnish. Strain and reserve the clam liquid.

Put the olive oil, garlic and bacon in the saucepan and cook over a medium heat until the bacon has browned. Add the onions, chilli, carrot and bay leaf. When the onion is translucent, tip in the potatoes, clam liquid and 250 ml (1 cup) of water. Cover and simmer for 35 minutes. Add the celery, clams and parsley and season with sea salt and white pepper. Ladle the chowder into four soup bowls and garnish with whole clams. Serves 4

mussels with rouille

2 kg (4 lb 8 oz) mussels
2 tablespoons olive oil
1 white onion, finely chopped
2 garlic cloves, crushed
3 large ripe tomatoes, diced
1 bay leaf
1 fennel bulb, finely sliced
1 pinch saffron threads
1 teaspoon sea salt
250 ml (1 cup) white wine
15 g (1/2 cup) flat-leaf (Italian) parsley leaves
rouille (basics)

Clean the mussels in the sink under cold running water, scrubbing them to remove any barnacles or bits of hairy 'beard'. Throw away any that are open and that do not close when you tap them.

Put the oil, onion and garlic into a large lidded saucepan and cook them over a low heat until the onions are transparent. Add the tomatoes, bay leaf, fennel and saffron, season with the sea salt and simmer for 10 minutes. Pour in the white wine, bring the sauce to the boil and tip in the mussels. Cover with the lid and cook for a few minutes, shaking the pan once or twice, then check that all the mussels have opened. Throw away any that remain closed.

Divide the mussels between four big bowls, sprinkle with the parsley and serve with the rouille and crusty white bread. Serves 4

buttered roast asparagus

3 tablespoons butter
2 bunches fine asparagus spears, ends trimmed
4 slices wholemeal toast
1 lemon
30 g (1/3 cup) shaved Parmesan cheese

Preheat the oven to 180°C (350°F/Gas 4). Put a roasting tin over a low heat and add the butter. When the butter has melted, add the asparagus and season with a little salt and pepper. Roll the asparagus around so that it is well coated in the butter and then put it in the oven to roast for 10 minutes.

Arrange the toast on four plates and top each with some asparagus. Squeeze a little lemon juice into the roasting tin, swirl it around and then drizzle the pan juices over the asparagus. Top with the Parmesan shavings. Serves 4

pea and lettuce soup

2 tablespoons olive oil
1 leek, finely sliced
1 garlic clove, crushed
1 litre (4 cups) vegetable or chicken stock
1 butter lettuce, stem removed, finely sliced
125 g (1 cup) fresh peas
1 teaspoon sugar
20 mint leaves
finely grated Parmesan cheese

Put the oil, leek and garlic into a large saucepan and sauté until the leek is soft. Add the stock, lettuce and peas and bring to the boil. Reduce the heat and simmer for 15 minutes or until the peas are soft, then remove the pan from the heat and add the sugar and mint leaves. Pour the soup mixture into a blender or food processor and whiz until it is smooth. Season well.

Serve the soup with some grated Parmesan to sprinkle over. Serves 4

lemon thyme roast chicken

1.8 kg (4 lb) chicken
1 bunch lemon thyme
3 lemons
1 white onion, quartered
2 tablespoons butter, softened

Preheat the oven to 200°C (400°F/Gas 6). Rinse the chicken and pat it dry with paper towels. Scatter some of the lemon thyme over the base of a roasting tin, then generously rub the chicken skin with salt and put it on top of the lemon thyme, breast-side-up.

Halve one of the lemons and put it inside the chicken, along with the onion quarters and some lemon thyme. Rub the softened butter over the breast and put the chicken in the oven for 1 hour and 15 minutes or until it is cooked through. Take the chicken out and check that it is cooked by pulling a leg away from the body — the juices that run out should be clear and not pink.

Squeeze the two remaining lemons over the chicken and put it back in the oven for a further 5 minutes. Remove the chicken from the oven and allow it to rest for 10 minutes before carving. Arrange the chicken pieces on a serving platter and pour some of the lemony pan juices over them. Serves 4

braised blue-eye cod

4 x 200 g (7 oz) blue-eye cod fillets or cod fillets
1 tablespoon olive oil
2 garlic cloves, thinly sliced
4 spring onions (scallions), thinly sliced
2 tablespoons finely chopped dill
250 ml (1 cup) white wine
1 lemon, zested and juiced
15 g (1/4 cup) roughly chopped flat-leaf (Italian) parsley
1 tablespoon butter
steamed snow peas (mangetout)

Rinse the fish fillets in cold water and pat them dry with paper towels, then rub them with salt and white pepper. Heat the oil in a nonstick frying pan and sauté the garlic until it is lightly golden, add the spring onions, dill, white wine, lemon zest and lemon juice and bring to the boil.

Add the fish and cover the pan, then reduce the heat and simmer for 8 minutes. Remove the fish pieces from the cooking liquid and arrange them on a warmed serving platter. Return the pan to a high heat and boil until the liquid has reduced by half, then add the parsley and butter, swirling the frying pan until the butter has melted, and pour the sauce over the fish.

Serve immediately with steamed snow peas. Serves 4

swordfish with a pine nut sauce

chicken and papaya salad

swordfish with a pine nut sauce

1 slice white bread, crusts removed
60 g (1/2 cup) pine nuts
1/2 garlic clove
2 tablespoons lemon juice
1 tablespoon olive oil
4 x 175 g (6 oz) swordfish steaks
salad of tomatoes, red onion and basil

Soak the bread in cold water and then squeeze it dry. Put the pine nuts, bread, garlic and lemon juice in a food processor and whiz to form a smooth paste, then add 60 ml (1/4 cup) water to thin it to a pourable consistency.

Heat the olive oil in a large frying pan over a high heat. Sear the swordfish steaks on one side for 2 minutes or until they are golden brown and then turn them over and reduce the heat. Cook the other side for a further 2 to 3 minutes or until the steaks are cooked through — they should feel firm when you press them.

Spoon the sauce over the fish and serve with a salad of tomatoes, red onion and basil. Serves 4

chicken and papaya salad

125 ml (1/2 cup) tamarind water
1 teaspoon soy sauce
2 teaspoons finely grated fresh ginger
1 tablespoon palm sugar
1/2 teaspoon cumin, roasted and ground
1 large red chilli, seeded and finely sliced
2 roast chicken breasts, roughly shredded
80 g (1/2 cup) peanuts, roughly chopped
1 orange papaya, peeled, seeded and sliced
1 Lebanese (small) cucumber, diced
2 tablespoons Asian fried onions
2 spring onions (scallions), shredded
20 g (1 cup) mint leaves
15 betel leaves

Mix the tamarind water, soy sauce, ginger, palm sugar, roast cumin and chilli together in a large bowl and keep stirring until the sugar has dissolved. Add the chicken to the dressing and toss it all together. Combine the remaining salad ingredients in another bowl and season.

Arrange the betel leaves and chicken on four plates and top with any remaining dressing. Serves 4

black bean salsa with tortillas

2 tablespoons olive oil
1 garlic clove, crushed
1 tablespoon ground cumin
1 red capsicum (pepper), finely diced
200 g (1 cup) fresh corn kernels
220 g (1 cup) cooked black turtle beans
25 g (1/2 cup) roughly chopped coriander (cilantro)
15 g (1/4 cup) roughly chopped mint leaves
1 tablespoon pomegranate molasses
finely chopped chipotle chilli or Tabasco sauce
rocket (arugula)
sour cream
tortillas

Put the olive oil in a frying pan over a moderate heat and add the garlic, ground cumin and diced red capsicum. Sauté until the capsicum is soft and then add the corn and black turtle beans. Cook for a further 5 minutes or until the corn is golden and soft, then remove the corn and bean mixture from the heat and tip it into a serving bowl. Add the remaining ingredients and season to taste with salt, pepper and the chipotle chilli or Tabasco sauce.

Serve with rocket, sour cream and warm tortillas, or as a side dish. Serves 4

fresh and fast

- Betel leaves are available from specialty Thai shops and make a great canapé base as well as a beautiful leafy addition to any salad. Serve topped with a fresh crab salad or small grilled prawns (shrimp) and mayonnaise.

- Toss diced red papaya in a dressing of lime juice, chilli, fresh coriander (cilantro) and finely sliced spring onions (scallions). Serve over roast duck.

- Barbecue fresh corn cobs and serve them with the charred husks pulled back, accompanied by a bowl of chipotle chilli or Tabasco-flavoured mayonnaise.

- Pomegranate molasses brings a bittersweet tang to any recipe and is ideal for adding to tomato-based salsas and sauces as well as to beetroot dip. Mix it with oil, thyme and sumac as a marinade for lamb fillets.

black bean salsa with tortillas

artichoke, bean and feta salad

eggplant and tofu salad

2 tablespoons white miso
1 tablespoon soy sauce
1 tablespoon sugar
1 tablespoon sesame oil
3 tablespoons oil
1 tablespoon finely grated fresh ginger
6 Japanese eggplants (aubergines), cut into chunks
2 red banana chillies, seeded and cut into rings
2 green banana chillies, seeded and cut into rings
400 g (14 oz) smoked tofu, cut into cubes
1 spring onion (scallion), finely chopped
1 tablespoon toasted sesame seeds

Mix the miso, soy sauce and sugar together while slowly adding 250 ml (1 cup) of water.

Heat both the oils together in a large frying pan or wok and add the ginger. As the ginger begins to sizzle, add the eggplant and toss until it is golden brown, then pour in the miso and soy mixture and simmer for 10 minutes. Add the banana chillies and cook for a further 2 minutes or until they are just beginning to soften.

Divide the tofu between four plates, top with the eggplant and garnish with the sliced spring onion and sesame seeds. Serves 4

watercress and duck salad

125 ml (1/2 cup) sherry
125 ml (1/2 cup) orange juice
1 tablespoon soy sauce
1 teaspoon sesame oil
1 teaspoon sugar
1 teaspoon finely grated fresh ginger
1 Chinese roast duck
110 g (4 oz) snow peas (mangetout), trimmed
400 g (1 bunch) watercress
1 x 200 g (7 oz) tin water chestnuts, drained and sliced

To make the dressing, put the sherry and orange juice into a small saucepan and bring to the boil, then reduce the heat and allow to simmer until the liquid has reduced by half. Pour it into a large bowl and add the soy sauce, sesame oil, sugar and ginger.

Remove the skin from the roast duck and cut it into thin strips, scraping off any fat. Lay the skin strips on a tray and grill them briefly until they crisp up, then put them on a paper towel to drain off any fat.

Remove the meat from the roast duck and tear it into strips before adding it to the bowl of dressing. Blanch the snow peas in boiling water and refresh them under cold running water.

Toss the duck meat with the watercress, water chestnuts, snow peas and crisp skin and serve. Serves 4

artichoke, bean and feta salad

4 globe artichokes
2 lemons, halved
4 tablespoons olive oil
8 mint leaves, finely chopped
250 g (8 oz) French beans, trimmed
110 g (4 oz) goat's feta cheese

Bring a large saucepan of salted water to the boil. Trim the artichoke stalks to within 2 cm (3/4 in) of the artichoke head, then pull away the outer leaves until the base of the leaves looks yellow and crisp. With a sharp knife, slice away the top third of the artichokes, scrape out the hairy central choke and pull out any of the spiky inner leaves. Rub the artichokes with the cut side of the lemon to stop them going brown. When the water is boiling, add the artichokes, weigh them down with a plate and simmer for 20 minutes.

Test that the artichokes are done by pushing the tip of a sharp knife into each one just above the stem — it should be tender. Drain the cooked artichokes upside down for a minute, then slice them in half. Put them in a large bowl with the olive oil, the mint and juice from the remaining lemon halves and season to taste.

Blanch the French beans in boiling water until they turn emerald green, then refresh under cold running water. Divide the artichokes between four plates, pile the beans on top and crumble on the feta. Drizzle with any remaining dressing. Serves 4

fresh and fast

- Serve a handful of watercress leaves with grilled polenta and crisp bacon.

- Melt Gruyère cheese over thickly sliced wholemeal toast and serve topped with a salad of baby rocket (arugula) leaves and marinated artichoke hearts.

- Serve fresh artichokes with grilled white fish and a dollop of garlicky aïoli.

- Finely slice a large eggplant (aubergine) and lightly fry it. Roll each eggplant slice around a spoonful of ricotta that has been flavoured with parsley, basil and a little Parmesan cheese. Bake the rolls for half an hour, then drizzle with a rich tomato sauce and serve with a green salad.

watercress and duck salad

asparagus with smoked salmon

1 egg yolk
1 teaspoon Dijon mustard
1 tablespoon lemon juice
1/2 teaspoon sugar
125 ml (1/2 cup) light olive oil
2 bunches asparagus, ends trimmed
30 g (1 cup) croutons (basics)
200 g (1/2 bunch) watercress, stalks removed
8 slices smoked salmon

Whisk together the egg yolk, mustard, lemon juice, sugar and a pinch of salt. Slowly add the olive oil, whisking until the mixture becomes thick and creamy. Set aside.

Bring a large saucepan of water to the boil. Cook the asparagus for 4 minutes or until it is tender, then refresh under cold running water. Drain the asparagus well. Put the dressing, asparagus, croutons and watercress into a large bowl and toss them all together. Divide the salmon between four plates, top with a pile of the salad and season with freshly ground black pepper. Serves 4

lamb cutlets with mint salsa

1 Lebanese (small) cucumber, finely diced
2 tablespoons finely diced red onion
2 tablespoons balsamic vinegar
1 tablespoon extra virgin olive oil
20 g (1 cup) mint leaves
1 tablespoon caster (superfine) sugar
1 tablespoon oil
12 small lamb cutlets
roast sweet potato (basics)

To make the salsa, put the cucumber, red onion, vinegar and olive oil in a small bowl and toss them together. Finely chop the mint leaves, sprinkling them with sugar halfway through chopping them. Add the mint and sugar to the bowl and stir them into the salsa.

Heat the oil in a frying pan and sear the lamb cutlets on one side until they are golden brown. Turn them over and cook the other side for another 2 to 4 minutes depending on how thick the cutlets are, then take the pan off the heat, season the cutlets and allow them to rest.

Divide between four plates and add some salsa to each cutlet. Serve with roast sweet potato. Serves 4

salmon fillets with a tamarind sauce

60 ml (1/4 cup) tamarind water
1 teaspoon fish sauce
1 teaspoon sesame oil
1 teaspoon soy sauce
1 teaspoon honey
4 x 140 g (5 oz) salmon fillets, skin removed
1 tablespoon sesame seeds
steamed rice
coriander (cilantro) leaves
lime wedges

Put the tamarind water, fish sauce, sesame oil, soy sauce and honey into a large glass or plastic bowl and stir together. Rinse the salmon fillets in cold water and pat them dry with paper towels, then add them to the tamarind mixture. Cover and marinate for an hour or overnight in the fridge.

Heat a nonstick pan over a high heat and sear the fillets, shaking off any excess marinade before you put them in the pan. When the fillets begin to brown, flip them over and reduce the heat.

Pour the remaining marinade into the pan and sprinkle the tops of the fillets with sesame seeds. Simmer the fillets for 5 to 8 minutes or until they are just cooked through and the marinade has reduced to a thick sauce. Serve with rice, coriander leaves and lime wedges. Serves 4

tamarind duck salad

4 duck breasts, thinly sliced across the grain
125 ml (1/2 cup) tamarind water
2 tablespoons grated fresh ginger
1 teaspoon Chinese five-spice powder
2 tablespoons palm sugar
115 g (4 oz) snow peas (mangetout)
1 tablespoon sesame oil
1 red capsicum (pepper), julienned
115 g (4 oz) bean sprouts
2 tablespoons toasted sesame seeds

Put the sliced duck breasts, tamarind water, ginger, five-spice powder and palm sugar into a bowl and leave to marinate for at least half an hour.

Blanch the snow peas in boiling water, refresh them under cold running water, then slice them in half lengthways. Heat a wok over a high heat. Put in the sesame oil, swirl the oil around the wok, add the marinated duck and stir-fry over a high heat for 5 minutes or until the duck is cooked. Remove the duck from the heat and allow it to cool a little before tossing it with the snow peas, capsicum and bean sprouts.

Deglaze the wok with the remaining marinade and allow it to simmer for 5 minutes. Pour this over the salad as a dressing and garnish with toasted sesame seeds. Serves 4

Freshly podded peas do taste different from the frozen option, evoking the flavour of spring and memories of favourite childhood meals.

lemon and thyme lamb cutlets

green pea curry

2 tablespoons oil
2 teaspoons brown mustard seeds
1 teaspoon grated fresh ginger
1 large white onion, thinly sliced
1 teaspoon ground cumin
1 teaspoon ground turmeric
1 red chilli, seeded and finely chopped
2 large ripe tomatoes, cut into chunks
2 tablespoons finely chopped mint
250 g (2 cups) fresh peas

Heat the oil in a deep frying pan and put in the mustard seeds. As the seeds begin to pop, add the ginger, onion and a little sea salt, and cook until the onion is soft. Mix in the cumin, turmeric and chilli, cook for a minute and then add the tomatoes and 125 ml ($1/2$ cup) of water. Simmer for 2 minutes and add the mint and the peas.

Cover and cook for 10 to 15 minutes, or until the peas are tender. Add the mint, season to taste and serve with steamed white rice. Serves 4

lemon and thyme lamb cutlets

1 bunch lemon thyme
12 lamb cutlets, French trimmed
60 ml ($1/4$ cup) lemon juice
60 ml ($1/4$ cup) olive oil
560 g (1 lb 4 oz) kipfler or salad potatoes
80 g ($3/4$ cup) black olives
15 g ($1/2$ cup) chopped flat-leaf (Italian) parsley
60 ml ($1/4$ cup) olive oil

Put half the bunch of lemon thyme into a container and lay the lamb cutlets on top. Cover with the remaining thyme, the lemon juice and the olive oil, making sure the cutlets are well coated in the marinade. Leave to marinate for at least an hour or preferably overnight in the fridge.

Cut the potatoes into big chunks, put them in a large saucepan of salted cold water and bring to the boil over a high heat. When the water has reached boiling point, cover the pan with a lid and remove it from the heat. Leave the potatoes to sit for half an hour. Take the cutlets out of the marinade and barbecue or grill them for 2 to 3 minutes on each side, then allow them to rest. Drain the potatoes and return them to the pan along with the olives, parsley and olive oil, stirring vigorously so that the potatoes are well coated and begin to break up a little. Season to taste. Serve the cutlets with the warm smashed potatoes and a green salad. Serves 4

chicken and preserved lemon salad

1 tablespoon sea salt
2 lemons, juiced
2 chicken breast fillets
3 tablespoons olive oil
1 teaspoon ground cumin
1 tablespoon finely chopped preserved lemon
90 g (1 cup) toasted almond flakes
50 g (1 cup) roughly chopped coriander (cilantro)
30 g (1/2 cup) roughly chopped mint
60 g (1/2 cup) sultanas

Bring a saucepan of water to the boil, add the salt, half the lemon juice and the chicken breasts, bring back to the boil, cover and remove from the heat. Leave the saucepan to sit for half an hour. Remove the chicken breasts from the water, drain them well and finely slice them against the grain.

Put the chicken in a large bowl and add the olive oil, ground cumin, preserved lemon, the rest of the lemon juice and the almond flakes. Toss them together briefly, then add the remaining ingredients and toss again. Serves 4

tuna with tomato and olives

10 cherry tomatoes, quartered
10 basil leaves
16 small black olives
1 tablespoon balsamic vinegar
2 tablespoons extra virgin olive oil
1 teaspoon olive oil
2 x 200 g (7 oz) tuna steaks

Put the tomatoes, basil leaves, black olives, balsamic vinegar and extra virgin olive oil into a bowl and mix.

Heat the olive oil in a frying pan over a high heat. Add the tuna steaks and sear them on one side for a minute. Turn the tuna steaks over, reduce the heat to medium and cook them for a further 3 to 4 minutes.

Put the tuna onto warmed plates and top with the tomatoes and olives. Serve with a green leaf salad. Serves 2

fish and saffron broth

2 teaspoons butter
1 large pinch saffron threads
1 onion, finely diced
2 garlic cloves, crushed
1 teaspoon finely grated fresh ginger
30 g (1 oz) ginger, peeled and cut into thin strips
6 ripe Roma (plum) tomatoes, diced
2 tablespoons tomato paste (purée)
1/2 teaspoon sea salt
4 spring onions (scallions), trimmed and cut into lengths
8 x 115 g (4 oz) pieces ling or firm white fish
20 g (1 cup) coriander (cilantro) leaves
crusty bread

Put the butter, saffron, onion, garlic and all the ginger into a large heavy-based frying pan and cook over a medium heat for 2 to 3 minutes until the onion becomes translucent. Add 500 ml (2 cups) of water, the tomatoes, tomato paste and salt and then simmer, covered, for 20 minutes. Put the spring onions and fish pieces into the tomato broth and cook, covered, for 7 minutes.

Divide the fish and broth between four pasta bowls and top with the coriander leaves. Serve with crusty bread. Serves 4

poached chicken with coriander

40 g (1 bunch) coriander (cilantro), washed well
3 lemons
1 tablespoon sea salt
4 chicken breast fillets
75 g (1/2 bunch) flat-leaf (Italian) parsley
1 garlic clove
125 ml (1/2 cup) olive oil
2 Lebanese (small) cucumbers, cut into chunks
leaf salad

Remove the roots and stems from the coriander and put them into a large pot of water. Add the juice of one lemon and the sea salt and bring to the boil. When the water is boiling, put in the chicken, cover the pot with a tight-fitting lid and remove it from the heat. Leave covered for an hour.

Meanwhile, to make the dressing put half the coriander leaves, parsley, garlic and the juice of the two remaining lemons into a blender or food processor. Blend everything together while slowly pouring in the olive oil. Season to taste.

When the chicken has cooked, drain it and slice it thinly across the grain. Toss the chicken with the dressing, cucumber and coriander leaves and serve with the leaf salad. Serves 4

(The chicken can be left to marinate in the dressing overnight in the fridge and tastes even better the next day.)

papaya and lemon grass syrup

pineapple fruit salad

papaya and lemon grass syrup

220 g (1 cup) sugar
2 stalks lemon grass, trimmed and bruised
125 ml (1/2 cup) passionfruit pulp
2 small red papayas

Put the sugar and lemon grass in a small saucepan with 250 ml (1 cup) of water, bring it to the boil, then reduce the heat and allow the mixture to simmer for 10 minutes or until it has reduced by half.

Add the passionfruit pulp and stir it in before taking the pan off the heat and allowing it to cool. This syrup will keep for several days in a sealed jar in the fridge. For added flavour, keep the lemon grass in the syrup until you are ready to use it.

Gently pour the syrup over the sliced papaya and serve either as it is or with lemon- or vanilla-flavoured ice cream. Serves 4

pineapple fruit salad

1 pineapple
10 mint leaves
2 teaspoons finely grated fresh ginger
1 teaspoon orange flower water

Skin the pineapple, cutting out any brown 'eyes'. Cut it into thin slices lengthways, trimming off any bits of woody core, and put the slices in a bowl along with the mint, ginger and orange flower water. Toss to combine, cover and allow to chill for an hour in the fridge.

Serve with coconut ice cream or honeyed yoghurt. Serves 4

mango and orange hearts

1 mango
1/2 lemon, juiced
6 leaves gelatine
110 g (1/2 cup) sugar
375 ml (1 1/2 cups) freshly squeezed orange juice
pouring cream
lime wedges

Purée the flesh of the mango with the lemon juice. Pour it into a measuring jug, ensuring that there is 250 ml (1 cup) of liquid. If it is a little under, top it up with water or orange juice. Set the purée aside.

Fill a large bowl with cold water and soak the gelatine leaves. Meanwhile, put the sugar and orange juice into a small saucepan. Heat, stirring, until the sugar has dissolved, then remove the saucepan from the heat and pour the juice into a bowl. Squeeze the water from the gelatine before putting the gelatine in the warm juice. Stir to dissolve and then add the puréed mango. Ladle the liquid into six small 100 ml (3 1/2 fl oz) heart-shaped moulds or ramekins and put them in the fridge for a few hours.

To remove the jellies from the moulds, dip the base of the moulds briefly in warm water and then turn the jellies out onto a plate. Serve with pouring cream and fresh lime wedges to squeeze over. Serves 6

fresh and fast

- Finely dice red papaya and fresh mango. Fold in a little mandarin syrup and layer with cream and slices of sponge cake.

- Serve wedges of chilled ripe pineapple with lime sorbet.

- While you are cooking a batch of pancakes, add a thin slice of pineapple to the uncooked top of each one, sprinkle with a little sugar and then flip the pancakes over. Serve with cream and fresh passionfruit.

- Slice fresh mango onto a plate, drizzle with a little coconut cream, and top with a crumble of palm sugar and toasted shredded coconut.

mango and orange hearts

mini mandarin cakes

The slightly perfumed flavour of mandarin gives an interesting twist to any dessert that calls for citrus zest or juice.

lemon and coconut tart

mini mandarin cakes

3 mandarins
6 eggs
145 g (2/3 cup) caster (superfine) sugar
180 g (13/4 cups) ground almonds
1 teaspoon baking powder
125 ml (1/2 cup) mandarin juice
55 g (1/4 cup) caster (superfine) sugar
poppy seeds

Preheat the oven to 180°C (350°F/Gas 4). Put the mandarins in a large saucepan and cover them with water, bring to the boil and cook for 2 hours. Drain the mandarins, allow them to cool, then break them into segments and take out any seeds.

Put the fruit and skin into a blender or food processor and purée them. Beat the eggs until light and fluffy, then add the sugar and beat for a further minute before folding in the ground almonds, baking powder and mandarin purée. Pour the mixture into 16 greased muffin tins and bake for 20 minutes.

Put the mandarin juice and sugar in a small saucepan, bring to the boil and simmer for 5 minutes or until the amount of liquid has halved. Remove the cakes from the tins, spoon over the mandarin syrup while they are still warm and sprinkle with poppy seeds.
Makes 16

lemon and coconut tart

125 g (41/2 oz) unsalted butter
345 g (11/2 cups) caster (superfine) sugar
4 large eggs
170 ml (2/3 cup) plain yoghurt
1 teaspoon natural vanilla extract
3 tablespoons lemon juice
2 tablespoons lemon zest
90 g (1 cup) shredded or desiccated coconut
1 prebaked shortcrust tart case (basics)
icing (powdered) sugar

Preheat the oven to 180°C (350°F/Gas 4). Beat the butter and sugar together until they are light and creamy. Add the eggs one at a time and beat them into the mixture before adding the yoghurt, vanilla, lemon juice and lemon zest. Stir in the coconut and pour the mixture into the prebaked tart case.

Bake for 30 minutes or until the filling is golden and puffed. Dust with icing sugar and serve warm with cream or ice cream.
Serves 8

almond macaroons with passionfruit

sticky pineapple cake

almond macaroons with passionfruit

2 large egg whites
230 g (1 cup) caster (superfine) sugar
230 g (2¼ cups) natural ground almonds
1 teaspoon natural vanilla extract
icing (powdered) sugar
crème fraîche
fresh passionfruit pulp

Preheat the oven to 180°C (350°F/Gas 4). Whisk the egg whites and sugar for about 5 minutes or until the mixture is light and fluffy, then fold in the ground almonds and vanilla extract.

Drop large spoonfuls of the mixture onto baking trays lined with baking paper and bake for 15 minutes or until the macaroons are pale brown. Allow the macaroons to cool before removing them from the baking tray.

Serve dusted with icing sugar and topped with crème fraîche and some fresh passionfruit. Makes 20

sticky pineapple cake

345 g (1½ cups) caster (superfine) sugar
180 g (2 cups) desiccated coconut, lightly toasted
250 ml (1 cup) coconut milk
280 g (1½ cups) diced fresh pineapple
4 eggs
250 g (2 cups) plain (all-purpose) flour
2 teaspoons baking powder
1 tablespoon unsalted butter, softened
125 g (1 cup) icing (powdered) sugar, sifted
2 tablespoons fresh lime juice

Preheat the oven to 180°C (350°F/Gas 4). Grease and line a round 24 cm (9½ in) springform tin. Put the sugar, coconut, coconut milk, pineapple and eggs into a large bowl and stir them together. Sift in the flour and baking powder and fold the ingredients together. Spoon the batter into the cake tin and bake for 1 hour.

Put the butter and icing sugar into a bowl and beat until you have worked the butter into the sugar. Slowly add the lime juice so that the icing is smooth and runny enough to be drizzled.

Test the cake with a skewer to see if it is cooked. Remove it from the tin, cool and then gently pour over the lime icing. Serves 8

strawberries with nutty filo

30 g (⅓ cup) flaked almonds
30 g (¼ cup) pistachio nuts
2 tablespoons honey
1 teaspoon grated lemon zest
1 tablespoon lemon juice
4 sheets filo pastry
2 tablespoons unsalted butter, melted
1 teaspoon cinnamon
icing (powdered) sugar
300 g (2 punnets) strawberries, hulled and halved
cardamom and rosewater syrup (basics)

Preheat the oven to 180°C (350°F/Gas 4). Finely chop the almonds and pistachios and put them in a small bowl along with the honey, lemon zest and juice. Put a piece of baking paper on a greased baking tray. Lay one of the filo sheets on top, brush the sheet with a little melted butter and then lay another sheet on top. Brush the top sheet with butter and sprinkle on the cinnamon and nut mixture. Top with two more buttered sheets of pastry.

Bake the filo for 15 minutes or until it is golden brown, then liberally cover the top with sifted icing sugar and break it into rough pieces.

Divide the strawberries between four plates. Top with the pastry and drizzle with some rosewater syrup. Serves 4

fresh and fast

• Quarter a punnet of strawberries, put them in a bowl with a dash of balsamic vinegar and fold the vinegar gently through the berries. Spoon the strawberries over a dollop of mascarpone and serve with a drizzle of Ligurian honey.

• Slice a banana in half lengthways, top with a large scoop of vanilla ice cream and drizzle with passionfruit syrup.

• Serve the nutty filo with finely sliced oranges sprinkled with Grand Marnier.

strawberries with nutty filo

summer

Summer is the season we most readily identify with fresh food. There's something about a sunny, relaxed state of mind that demands a casual approach to dining — bare feet, outdoor settings, big bowls piled with salads, the barbecue at the ready and icy drinks on hand. Life doesn't get much better than this, and neither does the seasonal produce: luscious stone fruit and berries, tropical exotica and salad basics. Summer cooking is all about great ingredients put together with ease and absolutely no fuss. There's no need to spend hours in the kitchen. Quality produce needs little more than the addition of roughly chopped herbs, some chilli, a splash of citrus. Stock up on extra virgin olive oil, good-quality vinegars, capers and olives, and fill the fridge with salad greens. Decorate the table with a bowl filled with summer colour: lemons, limes, avocados or mangoes. It doesn't come easier than that.

cucumbers

salad leaves

radishes

zucchini

tomatoes

capsicums

basil

sweetcorn

berries

apricots

passionfruit

peaches

plums

mangoes

nectarines

cherries

lychees

grapes

good ideas

salads

Beautiful leafy salads require a little attention to detail. Always buy loose leaves as you need them, since they rarely last very well in the fridge. If you are buying them in advance, always look for the perkiest whole lettuce. Rinse and remove any brown or wilting outer leaves before storing the lettuce in an airtight container that has been lined with a damp teatowel.

capsicums

Grilled red capsicums (peppers) add a luscious smoky sweetness to any summer salad. They can be marinated in oil, garlic, fresh herbs and, depending on the recipe, a sprinkle of ground cumin or paprika, then stored in the fridge ready for use. Cut into thick strips, they provide a quick and easy addition to any salad or grilled meat dish.

mango salsa

Salsas are a great way to bring the taste of summer to savoury dishes. Add diced mango to a bowl along with finely chopped spring onions (scallions), chillies, lime juice and a few drops of sesame oil and serve with grilled chicken. If you're not a chilli fan, toss the mango with some finely sliced red onion and cucumber. Season with freshly ground black pepper and a little lemon juice.

tomatoes

There's nothing more disappointing than a cold and tasteless tomato. So remember these two basic rules. Never refrigerate tomatoes, and always use them when they are a rich ruby red. Store tomatoes in a bowl on the kitchen counter and use them only when they've reached a ruddy ripeness.

berries

Berries and cream are a combination made in taste heaven. Serve strawberries in a bowl with whipped cream and broken meringue, or mash the berries with a little sugar and liqueur and pour the mixture over vanilla ice cream. Fill a bowl with mixed berries and toasted almonds and serve them with a jug of vanilla-tinged pouring cream.

cucumbers

Salting will draw much of the liquid from cucumber, resulting in a more intense flavour. Slice the cucumber into thin rounds or strips with a vegetable peeler and sprinkle with a little sea salt. Leave the cucumber for half an hour, squeeze to remove any excess liquid and then add the slices to a favourite salad or toss with a little dill and sour cream as an easy accompaniment for grilled salmon.

tamarind and squid salad

tomato with chilli and coriander

80 g (1 bunch) coriander (cilantro) leaves, roughly chopped
1 red onion, finely diced
2 large red chillies, seeded and finely chopped
1 teaspoon sea salt
3 tablespoons olive oil
1 tablespoon balsamic vinegar
4 large ripe tomatoes

Put the coriander, onion, chillies, sea salt, olive oil and balsamic vinegar in a bowl and toss them together.

Slice the tomatoes and arrange them on a plate. Scatter the coriander salsa on top, season and serve as a side dish or as a salad with a little seared tuna or fresh ricotta. Serves 4 as a side dish

tamarind and squid salad

1 tablespoon tamarind concentrate
1 tablespoon sugar
2 tablespoons fish sauce
1 tablespoon lime juice
1 garlic clove, crushed
1 small red chilli, seeded and julienned
4 medium squid (about 400 g/14 oz), cleaned
3 tablespoons oil
15 g (1/2 cup) basil leaves
15 g (1/2 cup) coriander (cilantro) leaves
90 g (1 cup) bean sprouts

To make the dressing, blend the tamarind with 60 ml (1/4 cup) of warm water, add the sugar, fish sauce, lime juice, garlic and chilli and stir until the sugar has dissolved.

Rinse the squid under cold running water and pat it dry with paper towels. Cut the tubes open down one side and lightly criss-cross the outside surface of the squid with score marks to make it curl up when you cook it. Heat the oil in a frying pan over a high heat and fry the squid tubes for 3 to 4 minutes on each side.

Cut each tube into bite-size pieces and toss them in the tamarind dressing with the herbs and sprouts. Serve with steamed white rice or rice noodles. Serves 4

risoni with sweet and sour capsicum

1 red onion, finely sliced
2 red capsicums (peppers), cut into thick slices
2 tablespoons balsamic vinegar
2 tablespoons brown sugar
250 g (9 oz) risoni
2 large ripe tomatoes, roughly chopped
10 large basil leaves, roughly torn
150 g (3 handfuls) baby rocket (arugula) leaves
4 tablespoons extra virgin olive oil

Preheat the oven to 180°C (350°F/Gas 4). Put the onion, capsicum, vinegar and sugar in a baking dish and toss them together. Season the vegetables with a little sea salt, cover with foil and bake in the oven for 30 minutes.

Remove the baking dish and allow the vegetables to cool. Cook the risoni in a large pan of rapidly boiling water for 10 minutes until it is *al dente*, then drain it well.

Put the risoni in a large bowl with the capsicum mixture, tomatoes, basil and rocket and toss to combine them. Season to taste and drizzle with olive oil. Serves 6

fresh and fast

- Toss sliced grilled capsicum (pepper) with anchovies, capers and basil for a quick pasta sauce or bruschetta topping.

- Dice ripe tomatoes and generously sprinkle them with salt. Set them aside for half an hour before adding olive oil, handfuls of roughly chopped parsley and fresh Parmesan cheese. Toss with warm pasta and sprinkle with small olives.

- Finely slice grilled capsicums (peppers) and toss them with fresh parsley, a few anchovies and some lemon zest. Serve with freshly grilled squid or octopus.

risoni with sweet and sour capsicum

jewelled gazpacho

4 Lebanese (small) cucumbers
8 ripe tomatoes, roughly chopped
1 tablespoon sea salt
1 teaspoon ground roast cumin seeds
1 small beetroot, peeled and chopped
1 red capsicum (pepper), diced
3 spring onions (scallions), finely sliced
1/2 red onion, finely diced
2 tablespoons chopped fresh coriander (cilantro) leaves

Roughly chop two of the cucumbers and finely dice the remaining two. Put the tomatoes and chopped cucumber into a large bowl with the sea salt and the ground cumin seeds, stir well and then leave to marinate for 2 hours. Tip the tomato and cucumber mixture into a blender or food processor with the beetroot and whiz to a purée.

Pour the purée into a muslin-lined strainer over a bowl, twist the muslin into a ball and squeeze out all the liquid. Discard the pulp and chill the juice.

When the juice is cold, add the diced vegetables and coriander and chill the gazpacho for a further hour. Season to taste, ladle into individual bowls and serve with a drizzle of extra virgin olive oil. Serves 4

grilled haloumi

250 g (9 oz) haloumi cheese
2 Lebanese (small) cucumbers
1/2 red onion, finely sliced
20 g (1 cup) mint leaves
1 tablespoon lemon juice
9 tablespoons olive oil

Slice the haloumi lengthways into eight thick slices. Trim the ends from the cucumbers, cut them in half and then again lengthways into long thin strips. Put the cucumber in a bowl along with the onion, mint leaves, lemon juice and 6 tablespoons of olive oil. Toss them together, season with salt and pepper and divide the salad between four plates.

Heat the remaining olive oil in a frying pan over a high heat and fry each of the haloumi pieces on both sides. Put the cheese on top of the salad and serve straight away. Serves 4 as a starter

ceviche salad

500 g (about 1 lb) white fish fillets
125 ml (1/2 cup) lime juice
60 ml (1/4 cup) coconut cream
1 teaspoon sugar
1 red capsicum (pepper), finely sliced
4 spring onions (scallions), thinly sliced on the diagonal
1 large red chilli, seeded and finely chopped
2 tomatoes, seeded and diced
2 avocados, diced
80 g (1 bunch) coriander (cilantro), roughly chopped

Slice the fish fillets into thin strips and put them in a glass bowl with the lime juice. Turn them over so that they are completely coated in the juice. Cover the fish and leave it to marinate and 'cook' in the fridge for 2 hours.

Drain the fish and toss it with the remaining ingredients. Divide the salad between four plates. Serves 4

steamed mussels with thai salsa

2 kg (4 lb 8 oz) mussels in the shell
500 ml (2 cups) white wine
2 tablespoons shaved palm sugar
1 tablespoon fish sauce
2 tablespoons fresh lime juice
1 red chilli, seeded and finely sliced
2 Lebanese (small) cucumbers, finely diced
1 tablespoon finely diced red capsicum (pepper)
15 mint leaves, finely sliced
lime wedges

Clean the mussels in a sink filled with cold water, removing the beards and any barnacles from the shell. Discard any mussels that remain closed and don't open when you tap them. Put them in a large lidded pot and pour over the wine. Cover with a tight-fitting lid and cook over a high heat, shaking the pan occasionally. Check after 4 minutes, removing any mussels that have opened. If any stay closed, return them to the heat for a minute, then discard any that still haven't opened. Allow the mussels to cool.

Put the palm sugar, fish sauce and lime juice in a small bowl and stir until the sugar has dissolved, then add the chilli, cucumber, capsicum and mint and mix them all together. Break the top shells off the mussels so that the meat is left sitting on a half-shell. Arrange the mussels on a serving platter with lime wedges and spoon the salsa into each one. Serves 4

snapper with a citrus dressing

seared prawns with mint and yoghurt chutney

snapper with a citrus dressing

2 oranges
1 lemon
2 limes
1/2 teaspoon pink peppercorns, roughly chopped
4 tablespoons light olive oil
2 tablespoons oil
4 x 200 g (7 oz) snapper fillets, skin on

Preheat the oven to 200°C (400°F/Gas 6). To make the dressing, zest the oranges, lemon and limes and put the zest into a bowl. Juice the lemon and add the juice to the bowl. Segment the oranges and limes and put them in the bowl along with any juice, then add the peppercorns and light olive oil and stir well.

Put the oil in a large ovenproof frying pan over a high heat. Rinse the snapper fillets in cold water and pat them dry with paper towels. Season the fillets liberally with sea salt and put them skin-side-down in the hot pan. Sear the fillets for a minute or two until the skin is crisply golden and then turn them over.

Put the pan into the oven and bake the snapper for 8 minutes, then transfer the fillets to a serving dish. Cover with the citrus dressing and serve immediately. Serves 4

salmon carpaccio

1 small fennel bulb
1/2 teaspoon sea salt
1 teaspoon finely chopped mint
1 teaspoon finely chopped dill
1 teaspoon sugar
1 lemon, juiced
310 g (11 oz) sashimi salmon, skin and bones removed
small salted capers
extra virgin olive oil

Cut the fennel bulb into paper-thin slices and finely chop the feathery fennel tops. Put the sliced fennel and fennel tops in a bowl along with the sea salt, chopped herbs, sugar and lemon juice and toss everything together. Cover the salad and put it in the fridge for at least an hour.

Check that all the bones have been removed from the salmon fillet before wrapping it in plastic wrap and putting it in the freezer for half an hour to firm it up. Cut the chilled salmon into paper-thin strips with a very sharp knife.

Divide the salmon slices between four small plates and top with the fennel salad, arranging it so that the salmon slices can be seen through the fennel. Sprinkle with some salted capers and drizzle with extra virgin olive oil. Serves 4

seared prawns with mint and yoghurt chutney

16 large raw prawns (shrimp), peeled and deveined
2 tablespoons olive oil
4 tablespoons lemon juice
15 g (1 cup) mint leaves
1 green chilli, seeded
1 teaspoon ground roast cumin
1 teaspoon sugar
1 tablespoon grated fresh ginger
5 tablespoons plain yoghurt
10 snow peas (mangetout), blanched
1 Lebanese (small) cucumber, diced
30 g (1 cup) coriander (cilantro) leaves

Toss the prawns in the olive oil and 1 tablespoon of the lemon juice. Put the mint leaves, 3 tablespoons of lemon juice, the green chilli, roast cumin, sugar and ginger into a blender and process to make a thin sauce. Pour the sauce into a bowl and fold through the yoghurt. Season to taste.

Heat a frying pan over a high heat and sear the prawns, a few at a time, until they are beginning to change colour and curl. Turn them over and cook them for a further minute on the other side.

Divide the snow peas, cucumber and coriander leaves between four plates and top them with the warm prawns. Drizzle with the chutney and serve with steamed white rice. Serves 4

fresh and fast

- Marinate prawns (shrimp) in lime juice and fresh ginger before throwing them on the barbecue.

- Blend yoghurt, grated fresh ginger, finely chopped mint and coriander (cilantro) together for an easy accompaniment to grilled salmon or ocean trout.

- Marinate thinly sliced salmon in lemon juice, ground cumin and a little olive oil. Serve as part of a salad or curled over sesame crisps for an easy canapé.

- Toss together grated fresh ginger, finely diced chilli, lime juice, ground cumin and diced fresh peaches for a summer salsa with a difference.

salmon carpaccio

74

Olives marinated with your favourite flavours make for easy pre-dinner nibbles.

fresh mozzarella salad

zucchini and caper spaghettini

3 tablespoons extra virgin olive oil
2 garlic cloves, crushed
6 zucchini (courgettes), grated
400 g (14 oz) spaghettini
15 g (1/2 cup) roughly chopped flat-leaf (Italian) parsley leaves
2 tablespoons small capers
110 g (4 oz) Parmesan cheese, grated

Bring a large saucepan of salted water to the boil for the pasta. Heat a deep frying pan over a medium heat and add the olive oil and garlic. Move the garlic around the pan with a spatula until it is lightly golden and then add the grated zucchini.

Slowly braise the grated zucchini, stirring it as it cooks, for about 15 minutes or until it begins to dry out and catch on the bottom of the pan.

Cook the pasta until it is *al dente* (about 10 minutes), then drain and return it to the saucepan. Add the parsley, capers, most of the Parmesan and the zucchini. Toss everything together and divide the pasta between four pasta bowls. Sprinkle with the remaining Parmesan. Serves 4

fresh mozzarella salad

4 x 125 g (4 1/2 oz) balls fresh mozzarella cheese
4 tablespoons virgin olive oil
120 g (1 bunch) sage
20 large black olives, pitted and quartered
1 orange, zested and juiced

Cut the mozzarella balls into thick slices and arrange them on four plates.

Put the oil in a frying pan over a high heat and add the sage leaves — as they begin to sizzle and darken, remove them from the oil and scatter them over the cheese. Gently pour a little of the oil over the mozzarella, then top with the olive quarters, orange zest and orange juice.

Serve with grilled focaccia or ciabatta. Serves 4 as a starter

mango salsa with black beans

1 x 170 g tin (3/4 cup) Chinese black beans
1 mango, diced
1 teaspoon ground cumin
1 large red chilli, seeded and finely chopped
3 tablespoons lime juice
1 teaspoon sesame oil
2 spring onions (scallions), finely sliced
15 g (1/2 cup) coriander (cilantro) leaves

Rinse the black beans, drain them and put them in a large bowl. Add the remaining ingredients, stir to combine them and season to taste.

Serve with barbecued chicken or as a side salad. You can make the salsa more substantial by adding bean sprouts and sliced cucumber. Serves 4 as a side salad

seared lime salmon with poppy seeds

4 x 170 g (6 oz) salmon fillets, skin on
3 limes
1 tablespoon soy sauce
3 tablespoons olive oil
3 tablespoons mirin
1 tablespoon poppy seeds
steamed rice

Preheat the grill. Rinse the salmon fillets in cold water and pat them dry with paper towels. Put the salmon in a bowl and add the juice of two of the limes, the soy sauce and the olive oil. Leave to marinate for half an hour.

Remove the skin from the remaining lime and slice it into paper-thin circles. Heat a large nonstick pan over a high heat and sear the salmon fillets, skin-side-up, for a minute. Turn each of the fillets over and take the pan off the heat.

Top the salmon fillets with the sliced lime and spoon over the mirin. Grill the fish for 3 to 4 minutes or until the salmon is cooked and the lime has caramelized. Sprinkle with the poppy seeds. Serve with steamed rice. Serves 4

octopus with thai dressing

2 red chillies, seeded and finely chopped
1 garlic clove, crushed
1 tablespoon grated palm sugar
1 tablespoon lime juice
3 tablespoons fish sauce
1 tablespoon rice wine vinegar
60 ml (1/4 cup) olive oil
2 tablespoons white wine vinegar
1 tablespoon finely chopped coriander (cilantro)
16 small octopus, cleaned
baby leaf salad
lime wedges

To make the Thai dressing, combine the chillies, garlic, palm sugar, lime juice, fish sauce and rice wine vinegar with 3 tablespoons of water and stir until the sugar has dissolved.

Mix the olive oil, vinegar and coriander together in a bowl and add the octopus. Cover and leave it to marinate for a few hours or preferably overnight in the fridge.

Take the octopus out of the marinade and grill it on a hot barbecue or grill plate for a few minutes on each side until it looks charred around the edges and is cooked through.

Serve the octopus on a baby leaf salad with the Thai dressing and a lime wedge. Serves 4 as a starter

thin-sliced beef with sesame

2 tablespoons hoisin sauce
2 tablespoons soy sauce
4 tablespoons sesame oil
3 tablespoons roasted sesame seeds
1 tablespoon honey
1 lime, juiced
1/2 teaspoon finely chopped chilli
700 g (1 lb 9 oz) roasted beef fillet
150 g (1 punnet) cherry tomatoes, quartered
2 Lebanese (small) cucumbers, finely sliced
1 small red onion, finely sliced
40 g (1/2 bunch) coriander (cilantro), leaves only

Combine the hoisin sauce, soy sauce, sesame oil, sesame seeds, honey, lime juice and chilli in a small bowl.

Finely slice the beef and put it in a large bowl. Add half of the sauce and the remaining salad ingredients and toss them together. Arrange the salad in piles on four plates and drizzle with the remaining sauce. Serves 4

squid and pine nut salad

fresh tomato and oregano salad

squid and pine nut salad

450 g (1 lb) small squid
4 anchovy fillets, finely chopped
2 tablespoons olive oil
1 lemon, zested and juiced
2 garlic cloves, crushed
150 g (3 handfuls) rocket (arugula) leaves
20 g (1 cup) parsley leaves
50 g shaved Parmesan cheese
80 g (1/2 cup) toasted pine nuts

Combine the squid, anchovy fillets, olive oil, lemon zest and garlic in a bowl and toss well to coat the squid thoroughly. Cover the squid and allow it to marinate for at least an hour.

Put a heavy-based frying pan over a high heat and cook the squid, searing it on both sides for 1 to 2 minutes, then pour on the marinade and cook for a further 30 seconds. Turn off the heat and allow the squid to sit for a few minutes before slicing it into thin rings. Put the squid in a bowl along with the remaining ingredients, dress with the lemon juice and toss together. Serves 4

fresh tomato and oregano salad

1 small white onion, halved and thinly sliced
1/2 tablespoon white sugar
1 tablespoon white wine vinegar
2 vine-ripened tomatoes
170 g (1 bunch) oregano, leaves only
extra virgin olive oil

Toss the onion and white sugar together and allow the mixture to stand for half an hour before adding the vinegar. Cut the tomatoes into eighths and sprinkle them with sea salt and freshly ground black pepper.

When you are ready to serve the salad, toss the tomatoes, onions and fresh oregano leaves together and serve with a trickle of extra virgin olive oil. Serves 4 as a side dish

soba noodle salad

4 tablespoons hijiki
1 teaspoon dashi granules
125 ml (1/2 cup) soy sauce
60 ml (1/4 cup) mirin
1 teaspoon sugar
4 spring onions (scallions), finely sliced on the diagonal
300 g (10 1/2 oz) soba noodles
1 tablespoon pickled ginger, finely chopped
500 g (1 lb 2 oz) daikon, julienned
1 Lebanese (small) cucumber, julienned
20 mint leaves, roughly torn

Soak the hijiki in warm water for 30 minutes and then drain it. Combine the dashi granules, soy sauce, mirin and sugar with 375 ml (1 1/2 cups) of water in a small saucepan and bring to the boil, stirring so that the sugar dissolves. Remove from the heat and allow the sauce to cool. Add the pickled ginger and finely sliced spring onions.

Cook the noodles in boiling water until they are *al dente*, then drain them and rinse with cold water to remove any starch.

Toss the noodles, daikon, hijiki, cucumber, mint and sauce together and divide between four bowls. Serve the salad as is, or top it with a small piece of teriyaki salmon or the spiced ocean trout on page 93. Serves 4

fresh and fast

• Finely slice a red onion and add 1 tablespoon of white wine vinegar and a teaspoon of sugar. Leave for an hour before adding parsley leaves, olive oil, finely sliced capsicum (pepper) and a few green peppercorns. Serve with grilled chicken.

• Make a quick sauce for white fish or prawns (shrimp) from mirin, mint leaves, freshly grated ginger and a little grape-seed oil.

• For a heartier version of the squid salad, blend all the ingredients except for the squid in a food processor with a drizzle of olive oil to form a rich sauce for the squid. Serve with boiled new potatoes.

soba noodle salad

green papaya salad

steamed fish with fresh herbs

2 stalks lemon grass, finely chopped
60 g (1/4 cup) caster (superfine) sugar
80 ml (1/3 cup) fish sauce
4 x 200 g (7 oz) white fish fillets, sliced into thick strips
1 red chilli, seeded and finely chopped
2 teaspoons finely grated fresh ginger
80 ml (1/3 cup) lime juice
1 tablespoon fish sauce
1 tablespoon palm sugar
10 g (1/2 cup) mint leaves
15 g (1/2 cup) coriander (cilantro) leaves
15 g (1/2 cup) basil leaves
3 Lebanese (small) cucumbers, cut into chunks

Put the lemon grass in a bowl with the sugar and fish sauce and add the fish pieces. Toss the fish in the sauce mixture to coat each piece well, and leave to marinate.

Put the chilli, ginger, lime juice, fish sauce and sugar in a bowl and stir until the sugar has dissolved. Add the fresh herbs and cucumber and put the salad on a serving platter. Put the fish pieces on a plate in a bamboo or metal steamer basket and put the basket over a saucepan of simmering water. Cover and steam for 3 to 4 minutes. Toss the fish gently through the salad while it is hot. Serves 4

couscous with herbs and chickpeas

185 g (1 cup) couscous
1 teaspoon butter
1 x 400 g (14 oz) tin chickpeas, drained and rinsed
2 ripe Roma (plum) tomatoes, seeded and diced
1/2 red onion, finely diced
10 g (1/2 cup) mint leaves
15 g (1/2 cup) coriander (cilantro) leaves
10 g (1/2 cup) flat-leaf (Italian) parsley leaves
1 tablespoon lemon juice
3 tablespoons olive oil
2 tablespoons diced preserved lemon

Put the couscous in a large bowl with the butter and cover with 250 ml (1 cup) of boiling water. Leave the couscous for 20 to 30 minutes, from time to time separating the grains with a fork. Before adding the remaining salad ingredients, rub the grains between your fingers to break up any lumps.

Toss the couscous and salad together and season with sea salt and freshly ground black pepper. Serves 4

green papaya salad

60 ml (1/4 cup) lime juice
3 tablespoons fish sauce
3 tablespoons sugar
2 large red chillies, seeded and finely chopped
1 tablespoon finely chopped mint
1 green papaya
2 tablespoons finely chopped roasted peanuts
15 g (1/2 cup) coriander (cilantro) leaves

To make the dressing, put the lime juice, fish sauce, sugar, chilli and fresh mint in a bowl and stir until the sugar has dissolved.

Peel the papaya and cut the flesh away from the stone in pieces. Finely julienne or grate the papaya and add it to the dressing along with the peanuts and coriander leaves.

Toss the salad ingredients together and serve immediately. Serves 4

fresh and fast

• For a slightly more aromatic twist on the papaya salad, replace the green papaya with green mango.

• If you have trouble finding preserved lemons, substitute Indian-style pickled lime or mango. Finely diced lime pickle also makes a great addition to any mayonnaise. Serve with barbecued prawns (shrimp).

• Toss diced tomato, preserved lemon and parsley together for a wonderful accompaniment to grilled fish or roast chicken.

couscous with herbs and chickpeas

sesame salad

4 tablespoons olive oil
1 tablespoon soy sauce
1 teaspoon sesame oil
2 tablespoons lime juice
1 teaspoon sugar
1 teaspoon finely grated fresh ginger
20 snow peas (mangetout), trimmed
140 g (5 oz) oyster mushrooms, quartered
30 g (1 cup) coriander (cilantro) leaves
1 red capsicum (pepper), julienned
2 spring onions (scallions), trimmed and finely sliced
1 large red chilli, seeded and finely chopped
3 tablespoons sesame seeds

To make the dressing, combine the olive oil, soy sauce, sesame oil, lime juice, sugar and ginger in a small bowl.

Blanch the snow peas in boiling water and refresh them under cold running water. Slice the peas in half lengthways and put them in a bowl with the oyster mushrooms, coriander leaves, red capsicum, spring onion and chilli, then add the dressing and toss everything together. Season to taste.

Heat a nonstick pan over a high heat, add the sesame seeds and lightly stir them around the pan until they are beginning to brown. Sprinkle the seeds over the salad. Serves 4

lamb fillet with cumin and tomato

2 large ripe tomatoes, cut into eighths
1/2 tablespoon sea salt
1 teaspoon ground roast cumin
1 tablespoon olive oil
1 red onion, halved and cut into wedges
1 tablespoon oil
500 g (1 lb 2 oz) lamb backstrap or loin fillet, trimmed
100 g (3 handfuls) spinach leaves

Preheat the oven to 180°C (350°F/Gas 4). Put the tomatoes in a baking dish and sprinkle them with the salt, cumin, olive oil and onion. Put the dish into the oven and bake for 20 minutes.

When the tomatoes are almost ready, put an ovenproof frying pan over a high heat and add a tablespoon of oil. Sear the lamb backstrap or fillet on all sides until it is well browned and then put it in the oven for 5 to 8 minutes, depending on how well done you like it.

Take the tomatoes and lamb out of the oven. Divide the spinach leaves between four plates and top them with the tomato pieces. Slice the lamb against the grain into thin slices, arrange them over the tomatoes, drizzle with the pan juices and season with black pepper. Serves 4

swordfish with green beans

3 tablespoons lemon juice
6 tablespoons extra virgin olive oil
1 garlic clove, crushed
1 tablespoon lemon thyme leaves
300 g (10 1/2 oz) green beans, trimmed
4 x 200 g (7 oz) swordfish steaks
2 tablespoons light olive oil

Mix the lemon juice, extra virgin olive oil, garlic and lemon thyme together in a small bowl.

Bring a large saucepan of salted water to the boil, drop in the green beans and cook them for 1 1/2 to 2 minutes, until they are emerald green and just cooked through. Drain and refresh under cold running water. Season the swordfish steaks liberally with sea salt.

Put the light olive oil in a large frying pan over a high heat. Add the swordfish steaks to the pan and sear them for 3 minutes or until golden brown. Turn them over, reduce the heat and leave them for a further 3 to 4 minutes or until they are cooked through. (You could barbecue them instead if you like.)

Put a swordfish steak on each plate and drizzle with the lemon thyme dressing. Top the fish with some green beans and season with freshly ground black pepper. Serves 4

pan-fried whiting

60 ml (1/4 cup) lemon juice
125 ml (1/2 cup) light olive oil
2 tablespoons finely chopped mint
2 tablespoons finely chopped dill
1 garlic clove, crushed
8 whiting fillets (about 500 g/1 lb 2 oz)
leaf salad
boiled new potatoes
lemon wedges

Put the lemon juice, olive oil, mint, dill and garlic into a large bowl and mix well. Rinse the whiting fillets in cold water and pat them dry with paper towels, then toss the fillets in the marinade, cover and leave them to marinate for a few hours in the fridge.

Heat a large nonstick frying pan over a high heat. Cook the whiting for 1 to 2 minutes on each side, then take the fillets out of the pan. Add any remaining marinade to the pan and cook for a minute. Serve the whiting on a leaf salad with quartered new potatoes, some of the pan juices and a lemon wedge. Serves 4

spiced ocean trout

Larger chillies like these are often sweeter and milder than the smaller ones, which tend to be more feisty and fiery.

coconut chicken salad

spiced ocean trout

560 g (1 lb 4 oz) ocean trout fillet, skin and bones removed
1 teaspoon sesame oil
4 spring onions (scallions), trimmed and cut into 3 cm
    (1 1/4 in) lengths
185 ml (3/4 cup) cider vinegar
55 g (1/4 cup) sugar
2 cm (3/4 in) piece fresh ginger, peeled and julienned
2 large red chillies, seeded and finely sliced
10 cm (4 in) piece young lemon grass, finely chopped
4 star anise
1 teaspoon Sichuan peppercorns
udon noodles

Cut the fish into 1 cm (1/2 in) wide slices and put them in a single layer in a large, deep, nonmetallic dish.

Put the sesame oil and the spring onions in a saucepan over a medium heat and cook them until the spring onions have turned a bright dark green. Pour 500 ml (2 cups) of water over the spring onions and mix in the vinegar, sugar, ginger, red chillies, lemon grass, star anise and peppercorns. Bring to the boil, stirring to make sure that the sugar has dissolved, and then pour the hot liquid over the ocean trout and leave it to cool.

Serve with udon noodles. Serves 4

coconut chicken salad

2 tablespoons finely chopped lemon grass
3 tablespoons lime juice
1 teaspoon palm or brown sugar
250 ml (1 cup) coconut milk
1 teaspoon sesame oil
2 chicken breast fillets
70 g (1 bunch) mint
1/4 fresh coconut, flesh shaved and toasted
100 g (1 handful) snow pea sprouts
2 Lebanese (small) cucumbers, finely sliced
2 tablespoons sesame seeds, toasted
lime wedges

Preheat the oven to 180°C (350°F/Gas 4). To make the dressing, combine the lemon grass, 2 tablespoons of lime juice, the palm sugar and coconut milk in a small saucepan over a low heat. Simmer for 10 minutes, stirring occasionally to ensure that the sugar has dissolved, then remove from the heat and allow to cool.

Put the sesame oil and 1 tablespoon of lime juice into a small bowl. Add the chicken breasts and toss them in the oil and juice before putting them in a baking dish. Drizzle the chicken with the remaining marinade, cover with foil and bake in the oven for 30 minutes. Remove the chicken and allow it to cool completely. Roughly shred the chicken and add it to the bowl with the dressing. Add the remaining salad ingredients and toss everything together with the sesame seeds. Serve with a wedge of lime. Serves 4

salad of avocado and preserved lemon

2 avocados
3 Lebanese (small) cucumbers
2 tablespoons finely chopped preserved lemon
50 g (1 cup) roughly chopped coriander (cilantro)
2 tablespoons virgin olive oil
1 tablespoon lemon juice

Remove the skin and stone from the avocados and cut into bite-size chunks. Halve the cucumbers lengthways and slice them into thick pieces on the diagonal.

Put the avocado, cucumber, preserved lemon, coriander, olive oil and lemon juice in a bowl and lightly toss them together without breaking up the avocado.

Serve with grilled fish or as a side salad. Serves 6 as a side dish

fattoush

1 garlic clove, crushed
1 teaspoon sea salt
4 tablespoons lemon juice
4 tablespoons extra virgin olive oil
3 ripe tomatoes, cut into wedges
2 tablespoons sumac
1 1/2 medium-size pitta breads
125 ml (1/2 cup) light olive oil
1 telegraph (long) cucumber, peeled, seeded, halved
   and thickly sliced
5 spring onions (scallions), thinly sliced at an angle
6 red radishes, thinly sliced
50 g (1 handful) baby rocket (arugula) leaves
20 g (1 cup) flat-leaf (Italian) parsley leaves
10 mint leaves, roughly chopped
1 cos (romaine) lettuce, roughly chopped

Put the garlic, salt, lemon juice and olive oil into a large bowl with the tomatoes and sumac and stir them together. Slice or tear the pitta bread into bite-size pieces and fry them in the olive oil over a medium heat until they are golden brown. Remove the fried bread pieces with a slotted spoon and drain them on paper towels.

Add the chopped cucumber, spring onions, radishes, rocket, herbs and lettuce to the bowl of tomatoes and just before serving toss the fried bread through the fattoush. Serves 4

smoked trout and cucumber salad

2 telegraph (long) cucumbers, peeled and seeded
1 tablespoon sea salt
1 smoked rainbow trout (about 250 g/9 oz)
1 teaspoon sugar
1 tablespoon lemon juice
30 g (1 bunch) chives, finely chopped
125 ml (1/2 cup) cream
1 tablespoon finely chopped dill
400 g (1 bunch) watercress, broken into sprigs

Finely slice the cucumbers, sprinkle them with the sea salt and leave them to drain in a colander for 30 minutes.

Take the skin off the trout and flake the flesh, making sure that you remove all the small bones. Squeeze any liquid from the cucumber slices and put them in a large bowl along with the smoked trout.

Blend together the sugar, lemon juice, chives, cream and fresh dill, pour the dressing over the cucumber and trout, then toss to combine. Divide the watercress leaves between four plates and top them with the cucumber and trout salad. Serves 4

fennel salad

2 tablespoons balsamic vinegar
4 tablespoons olive oil
1 teaspoon Dijon mustard
2 fennel bulbs, finely sliced
2 oranges, segmented
20 g (1 cup) flat-leaf (Italian) parsley leaves
30 g (1/4 cup) walnuts, roughly chopped
20 Niçoise olives

Put the vinegar, oil and mustard in a small bowl and stir to combine. Toss the fennel, orange, parsley, walnuts and olives together in a large serving bowl and drizzle with the dressing. Serves 4 as a side dish

blackberry fool

drunken grapes

500 g (1 lb 2 oz) green seedless grapes
3 tablespoons brown sugar
4 tablespoons vodka
4 tablespoons crème fraîche
45 g (1/2 cup) toasted almond flakes

Slice the grapes in half and put them in a nonmetallic bowl. Add the brown sugar, vodka and crème fraîche and stir them all together. Cover the grapes with plastic wrap and refrigerate them for several hours.

Spoon the chilled grapes into four dessert bowls and top with the toasted almonds. Serves 4

blackberry fool

300 g (10 1/2 oz) blackberries
3 tablespoons caster (superfine) sugar
2 tablespoons crème de framboise (optional)
1 teaspoon orange flower water
315 ml (1 1/4 cups) cream, whipped

Put the blackberries, sugar, liqueur and orange flower water into a blender or food processor and whiz to a purée (if you don't like seeds, sieve the purée at this point).

Fold the puréed berries into the cream and spoon the mixture into four chilled glasses.

Serve the fool with almond bread or biscotti. Serves 6

white peach ice cream

3 large white peaches, stoned and peeled
3 tablespoons Cointreau
2 tablespoons lemon juice
1 teaspoon rosewater
4–6 tablespoons caster (superfine) sugar
315 ml (1 1/4 cups) cream, whipped
45 g (1/2 cup) toasted almond flakes

Cut the peaches into small cubes and mix them with the liqueur, lemon juice, rosewater and caster sugar, stirring until the sugar dissolves.

Fold the fruit mixture into the whipped cream, then stir in the almonds. Pour the mixture into a 22 x 8 x 7 cm (9 x 3 x 2 3/4 in) terrine or mould and freeze it overnight.

Unmould the terrine by dipping it briefly into hot water before turning it out. Serve the ice cream in slices on chilled plates. Serves 6

fresh and fast

• Serve biscotti or almond bread with double cream and finely sliced white peaches seasoned with a little ground black pepper.

• Depending on availability, substitute the blackberries with any combination of your favourite berries for a mixed berry fool.

• Blend raspberries, white peaches and orange juice with a handful of crushed ice for the perfect summer afternoon drink.

• A classic summertime favourite is fruit salad made from freshly sliced yellow peaches, sliced bananas, passionfruit and the juice of an orange or lime. Serve with ice cream.

white peach ice cream

lemon and mint granita with shaved melon

Slices of chilled melon will cool down any hot summer afternoon and provide the perfect base for a quick fruit whip or cocktail.

hazelnut meringue with berries

lemon and mint granita with shaved melon

230 g (1 cup) caster (superfine) sugar
250 ml (1 cup) lemon juice
1 teaspoon orange flower water
10 mint leaves, finely chopped
1/4 each of 1 champagne melon and 1 seedless watermelon

Put the sugar in a saucepan with 500 ml (2 cups) of water and heat until the sugar has dissolved. Stir in the lemon juice, orange flower water and mint leaves and pour the mixture into a large plastic container. Freeze the granita for 3 hours, then break it up with a fork and re-freeze it.

Slice the melons into very thin slices. Alternating the two kinds of melon, make a small stack of slices on each of six plates. Take the granita out of the freezer, break it up with a fork again and spoon it over the melon. Serves 6

hazelnut meringue with berries

2 egg whites
115 g (1/2 cup) caster (superfine) sugar
4 tablespoons ground hazelnuts
310 ml (1 1/4 cups) whipping cream
1 teaspoon natural vanilla extract
3 punnets (about 450 g/1 lb) mixed strawberries, raspberries and blackberries, strawberries quartered

Preheat the oven to 150°C (300°F/Gas 2). Whisk the egg whites until they form soft peaks and then slowly add the sugar, continuing to beat until the mixture is stiff. Fold in the ground hazelnuts.

Line two baking trays with baking paper and divide the meringue between them, putting a big dollop in the middle of each tray. Using the back of a spoon, spread the mixture out until you have two 20 cm (8 in) circles of meringue.

Bake for 40 minutes. Turn the oven off, but leave the meringues in the oven, with the door ajar, for half an hour.

Whip the cream and fold in the vanilla extract. When the meringues are cool, put one of the rounds on a serving plate and top with some of the cream and half the berries, arranging them so that they make a flat surface for the next meringue layer. Put the other meringue on top and decorate with the cream and remaining berries. Allow to sit for 15 minutes before serving. Serves 6

nectarine salad

marinated plums with toasted Madeira cake

nectarine salad

8 nectarines, stones removed, sliced into eighths
150 g (1 punnet) raspberries
1 tablespoon grated fresh ginger
45 g (1/4 cup) brown sugar
1 lime, juiced

Put all the ingredients into a large bowl and gently toss them together. Allow the salad to marinate for an hour.

Serve with crème fraîche or plain yoghurt. Serves 6

marinated plums with toasted madeira cake

400 g (14 oz) ripe plums, stones removed, finely sliced
2 tablespoons caster (superfine) sugar
1/2 vanilla bean, finely chopped
6 tablespoons dessert wine
4 slices Madeira (pound) cake

Put the finely sliced plums, sugar, vanilla bean and dessert wine into a bowl. Stir, then cover the bowl with plastic wrap and put it in the fridge for several hours until you are ready to serve.

Take the plums out of the fridge. Grill the slices of Madeira cake on both sides until they are lightly browned.

Put the slices of cake on dessert plates, top with the marinated plums, drizzle with the remaining juice and serve with a scoop of vanilla ice cream. Serves 4

peach and blueberry shortcake

60 g (1/2 cup) plain (all-purpose) flour
30 g (1/4 cup) cornflour
45 g (1/4 cup) brown sugar
1/2 teaspoon ground ginger
1/2 teaspoon baking powder
1 1/2 tablespoons unsalted butter, softened
1 egg yolk
150 g (1 punnet) blueberries
2 tablespoons caster (superfine) sugar
2 peaches, peeled and sliced
icing (powdered) sugar
thick cream

Preheat the oven to 180°C (350°F/Gas 4). Sift the flours, sugar, ginger and baking powder into a bowl, then work in the butter and the egg yolk to form a soft dough. If the dough is too stiff, add a splash of cold water. Roll out the pastry and cut it into four 8 cm (3 in) rounds.

Put the pastry on a baking tray lined with baking paper. Bake for 12 minutes or until golden brown. Leave to cool. Heat a nonstick pan over medium heat and add the blueberries, 2 tablespoons of water and the caster sugar. Heat until the sugar has melted and the berries look glossy and their skins start to split. Arrange the shortbread on four plates with the peaches on top, spoon over the berries and dust with icing sugar. Serve with thick cream. Serves 4

fresh and fast

• Poach plums in orange juice with cinnamon or vanilla and serve them chilled with whipped cream and plain chocolate biscuits.

• Sprinkle nectarine halves with sugar and put them under a hot grill until the sugar has melted. Serve in a pile with pistachio ice cream.

• Blend raw sugar with a vanilla bean to form a fine powder, then sprinkle this over a bowl of blueberries. Toss with a dash of Cointreau and serve the blueberry mixture layered with whipped cream and raspberries in chilled glasses.

peach and blueberry shortcake

autumn

As the first golden leaves appear on the trees and a chill tinges the early morning air, heralding the cold months ahead, it's time to start thinking about warm comfort food. Which in no way means turning our backs on fresh produce. This is the season when all the deeply delicious root vegetables are harvested, a time when food has a distinctly woodland feel about it. Seek out the distinctive flavours of autumn: the earthiness of mushrooms, eggplant and beetroot and the fruity richness of quinces and figs. Start thinking of creamy, flavourful cheeses, walnuts, pecans, freshly sliced pears, warm greens, roasted pumpkin and the spicy sweetness of cinnamon. Decorate the table with autumn leaves and echo the mellow mood of the season in your settings, using textured natural fabrics and organic ceramics in shades of warm brown and russet.

pumpkins

beetroot

witlof

mushrooms

celeriac

fennel

olives

spinach

daikon

leeks

onions

sweet potatoes

pomegranates

pears

nuts

figs

oranges

quinces

good ideas

beetroot

Marinate baked beetroot in a little oil flavoured with garlic and pomegranate molasses. If you are cooking baby beetroot, reserve the smaller leaves for garnishing. Purée roast beetroot with some roast garlic and seasoning and serve as an accompaniment to grilled lamb or beef.

fennel

If you love the flavour and texture of uncooked fennel, invest in a small slicer which will deliver paper-thin slivers — these will add a light crunch to any warm salad. Marinate fennel slices in extra virgin olive oil, lemon juice and pitted olives and serve them with grilled white fish.

quinces

Stir any extra syrup from baked quinces into thick (double/heavy) cream or custard to add a sweet, perfumed tang. Make a syrup from the discarded skins by simmering them in a sugar syrup with vanilla or cinnamon. Strain and use the syrup to poach pears or to pour over a basic sponge or chocolate cake.

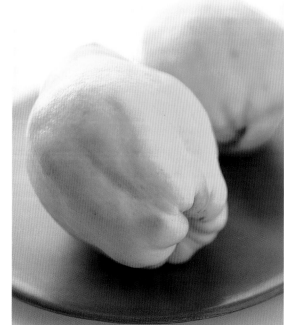

mushrooms

Finely slice button mushrooms and marinate them in olive oil, a little balsamic vinegar, garlic and finely chopped parsley. Serve as a side dish or spooned over bruschetta. Or fill the caps of field mushrooms with finely chopped prosciutto and tomatoes, bake and serve alongside scrambled eggs for a warming Sunday brunch.

celeriac

Grate celeriac and toss it through some lemon mayonnaise with a healthy blob of mustard and a handful of roughly chopped flat-leaf (Italian) parsley. Serve with sliced sourdough toasts. Roughly chopped chunks of celeriac make a great addition to your roast vegetable selection.

eggplants

Slice eggplant (aubergine) into thin slivers and fry them as chips to serve with spiced yoghurt and hummus. For a rich pasta sauce, cut eggplant into chunks and lightly fry it with garlic, red capsicum (peppers) and a late addition of tinned tomatoes.

smoked trout fishcakes with wilted spinach

smoked trout fishcakes with wilted spinach

2 medium potatoes, peeled
2 spring onions (scallions), finely sliced
200 g (7 oz) smoked trout, skin and bones removed
75 g (1 bunch) dill, finely chopped
2 tablespoons finely chopped chives
1 egg
60 ml (1/4 cup) oil
2 tablespoons butter
750 g (2 bunches) English spinach, washed
lemon halves

Cut the potatoes into chunks. Put them in a saucepan of salted cold water, bring them to the boil and then cook at a simmer until they are tender. Drain and mash the potatoes.

Add the spring onions, smoked trout, dill and chives to the mash, mix them together, season and then stir in the egg. Form the mixture into 16 patties.

Heat the oil in a frying pan and cook the patties in batches until they are golden brown and crisp on both sides. Drain them on paper towels.

Heat the butter in another pan and sauté the spinach for about a minute, so that it is just wilted. Pile the spinach onto four plates and add the fishcakes. Serve with lemon halves. Serves 4

pine mushroom salad

2 garlic bulbs
3 tablespoons extra virgin olive oil
1 tablespoon balsamic vinegar
4 large pine mushrooms
2 tablespoons light olive oil
40 g (1/4 cup) toasted pine nuts
150 g (1 bunch) flat-leaf (Italian) parsley, roughly chopped
40 g (1/3 cup) shaved Parmesan cheese
1 sourdough baguette

Preheat the oven to 200°C (400°F/Gas 6). Wrap the garlic bulbs in foil and bake them in the oven for half an hour until the cloves are soft and a little mushy. Slice the garlic in half and squeeze the soft cloves into a small bowl. Mash the garlic with a fork, then add the olive oil and vinegar and season with a little salt, white pepper and a pinch of sugar. If the sauce is quite thick, add 2 tablespoons of hot water to thin it down.

Meanwhile, brush the mushrooms with a little oil and bake them in the oven for 20 minutes, until they are just beginning to soften. Slice half of them. Put the mushrooms in a bowl with the pine nuts and parsley, add the garlic dressing and lightly toss the salad before piling it onto individual plates or a serving platter. Top with the Parmesan and serve with thinly sliced and toasted sourdough bread. Serves 4

baked eggs

1–2 tablespoons butter, softened
4 slices prosciutto, finely chopped
4 tablespoons finely chopped parsley
8 eggs
2 tablespoons grated Gruyère cheese

Preheat the oven to 180°C (350°F/Gas 4). Generously butter four 8 cm (3 in) ramekins and put them into a roasting tin half-filled with water.

Divide the prosciutto and parsley between the ramekins. Put the eggs into a bowl, season and then lightly whisk them together. Fill the ramekins with the egg mix, sprinkle with the cheese and put the roasting tin into the oven. Bake for 25 to 30 minutes, by which time the egg should be just set.

Serve with buttered toast. Makes 4

fresh and fast

- Finely slice pine mushrooms, field mushrooms and oyster mushrooms and sauté them with some butter, garlic and prosciutto. Add to *al dente* pasta with a scattering of fresh oregano leaves and shaved Parmesan cheese.

- Add thickly sliced field mushrooms to any beef stew to give some additional rich meaty flavour.

- Make a lemon mayonnaise flavoured with dill and serve it with seared salmon and boiled new potatoes.

- The baked eggs can have any number of ingredients added to them. Try removing the prosciutto and replacing it with capers and lots of parsley, and serve topped with a curl of smoked salmon. Alternatively, add some finely chopped bacon, spring onion (scallion) and basil, and serve with oven-roasted tomatoes.

pine mushroom salad

red onion tart

1½ sheets butter puff pastry
1½ tablespoons butter
1 large pinch saffron threads
1 kg (2 lb 4 oz) red onions, finely sliced
125 ml (½ cup) white wine
1 heaped teaspoon sea salt
1 teaspoon cracked black pepper
4 egg yolks
250 ml (1 cup) thick (double/heavy) cream
50 g (½ cup) grated Parmesan cheese

Preheat the oven to 180°C (350°F/Gas 4). Line a 25 cm (10 in) flan tin with the pastry and chill until you need it.

Heat the butter and saffron in a large frying pan over a medium heat. Add the onions and cook, stirring often, until they are soft and transparent. Pour in the white wine, cover the pan and simmer on a low heat for a further 40 minutes or until the onions are buttery soft and slightly caramelized.

Prick the pastry base with a fork and bake it blind for 15 minutes. Remove the baking weights and bake for 5 to 10 minutes more, until the base is golden. When the onions are cooked, add the salt and pepper and then tip them into the tart case. Whisk the yolks and cream together and pour them over the onions. Sprinkle on the Parmesan and bake for 30 minutes until the filling has set and is golden brown. Serve with a salad of bitter leaves. Serves 8

beetroot and goat's cheese salad

4 large beetroot
400 g (14 oz) butternut pumpkin (squash), cut into bite-size chunks
3 tablespoons olive oil
75 g (½ cup) hazelnuts
1 tablespoon balsamic vinegar
1 teaspoon brown mustard seeds
240 g (2 bunches) rocket (arugula)
200 g (7 oz) goat's cheese

Preheat the oven to 180°C (350°F/Gas 4). Put the unpeeled beetroot into a roasting tin with 250 ml (1 cup) of water. Cover the tin with foil and bake for 1 hour or until a knife will pass easily through the beetroot. Remove the beetroot and leave to cool.

Toss the pumpkin in 2 tablespoons of the olive oil, season well and roast for 15 minutes or until it is pale brown and cooked through. Roast the hazelnuts for 5 minutes and allow them to cool before rubbing away their skins.

Peel the skins from the beetroot — they should simply slip free, but it is a good idea to wear rubber gloves in case you need to rub the skins off. Slice the beetroot into eighths lengthways.

Mix the vinegar, remaining olive oil and mustard seeds. Put the beetroot, pumpkin, hazelnuts and rocket in a bowl, toss with the dressing and season well. Serve in a large bowl with the goat's cheese crumbled over the salad. Serves 4–6

roast pumpkin with tahini

900 g (2 lb) butternut pumpkin (squash)
1 tablespoon oil
3 tablespoons tahini
125 ml (½ cup) plain yoghurt
1 teaspoon ground roast cumin
½ teaspoon finely chopped garlic
1 tablespoon lemon juice
120 g (1 bunch) rocket (arugula)
20 g (1 cup) flat-leaf (Italian) parsley leaves
1 tablespoon black sesame seeds

Preheat the oven to 180°C (350°F/Gas 4). Peel the pumpkin and cut it into large chunks. Toss it in the oil, season with sea salt and freshly ground black pepper and then put the chunks on a baking tray. Roast for 30 minutes or until the pumpkin is tender, then allow it to cool.

To make the dressing, mix the tahini, yoghurt, cumin, garlic and lemon juice to a smooth paste and then season to taste.

Toss the rocket and parsley leaves together and pile them onto a serving platter. Top with the roast pumpkin, add a spoonful of the dressing and then garnish with a sprinkling of black sesame seeds. Serves 4 as a side dish

squid salad with red capsicum and curry vinaigrette

2 red capsicums (peppers)
10 large basil leaves, roughly torn
1 tablespoon lemon juice
1 teaspoon brown sugar
1 teaspoon curry powder
5 tablespoons extra virgin olive oil
500 g (1 lb 2 oz) small squid, cleaned
100 g (3 handfuls) baby spinach leaves

Roast the capsicums in a hot oven — 200°C (400°F/Gas 6) — or over a gas flame until the skin blisters, then put them in a plastic bag or covered bowl and allow them to cool. When they have cooled, peel away the skin, take out the seeds and finely slice the flesh. Put the sliced capsicum in a large bowl with the basil leaves. Blend together the lemon juice, brown sugar, curry powder and 4 tablespoons of the olive oil and pour this over the capsicum. Season to taste.

Heat a large frying pan over a high heat, add the remaining olive oil and sear the squid for 2 minutes on each side or until it is cooked. Slice the squid into thick rings before adding it to the capsicum. Toss the spinach leaves through the salad and season to taste. Serves 4

tapenade linguine

pear and walnut salad

100 g (^{1}/$_2$ cup) walnut halves
^{1}/$_2$ garlic clove
1 teaspoon sea salt
1 orange, zest grated, juiced
125 ml (^{1}/$_2$ cup) light olive oil
240 g (2 bunches) rocket (arugula)
2 beurre bosc pears
140 g (5 oz) goat's curd

Put the walnuts, garlic, sea salt, grated orange zest and olive oil in a blender or food processor and whiz to form a sauce. Toss the rocket leaves in the orange juice and divide the leaves between four plates.

Core the pears, slice them thinly and arrange the slices over the rocket. Top with the goat's curd, gently pour the walnut dressing over the salad and season. Serves 4 as a starter

tapenade linguine

30 g (1 cup) roughly chopped flat-leaf (Italian) parsley
45 g (^{1}/$_4$ cup) pitted and chopped black olives
1 lemon, zested
4–6 anchovies, finely chopped
1 tablespoon salted capers, rinsed
70 g (2^1/$_2$ oz) shaved Parmesan cheese
60 ml (^{1}/$_4$ cup) extra virgin olive oil
400 g (14 oz) linguine

To make the tapenade, put the parsley, olives, lemon zest, anchovies, capers, Parmesan and olive oil into a large bowl and toss them together.

Cook the pasta in boiling water until it is *al dente*, then drain and return it to the warm saucepan. Add the tapenade, toss it through the linguine and divide between four warm pasta bowls. Serves 4

field mushrooms on puff pastry

4 field mushrooms
2 tablespoons olive oil
1 garlic clove, crushed
1 sheet butter puff pastry
120 g (1 bunch) rocket (arugula)
70 g (2^1/$_2$ oz) shaved Parmesan cheese
1 tablespoon balsamic vinegar

Preheat the oven to 180°C (350°F/Gas 4). Remove the stem from each of the mushrooms and put the caps into a large bowl with the olive oil, garlic and some sea salt and freshly ground black pepper. Coat the mushrooms in the garlicky oil.

Cut the butter puff into four squares and lay them on a baking tray. Roll the edges of each square over to form a raised edge, then put a mushroom into the centre of each pastry square. Bake for 20 minutes or until the pastry is puffed and golden.

Tear the rocket leaves into bite-size pieces, toss them with the Parmesan and vinegar and season to taste. Pile the rocket salad on top of the mushroom tartlets and serve them while they are still warm. Serves 4

fresh and fast

- Finely slice some pears, toss them through a simple salad of rocket (arugula) and Parmesan cheese and dress with a balsamic vinaigrette.

- Process walnuts, garlic and parsley together to form a thick paste and use the mixture to stuff a beef fillet, or add a little light olive oil to the paste and serve it as a sauce with seared lamb fillets.

- The rough tapenade mixture used as a base for the linguine is also ideal as a quick accompaniment for barbecued steak.

- Place 8 field mushrooms in a baking dish with some finely chopped garlic and fresh thyme. Bake for half an hour, then remove the mushrooms and blend them with a little vegetable stock and a dash of cream. Season with salt and white pepper. Serve the soup hot with a scattering of fresh parsley and some buttery toast.

field mushrooms on puff pastry

farmhouse cheese with pomegranate and radicchio

The exquisite pomegranate is ideal for decorating an autumn table. Its juice, mixed with a little orange, is a great basis for an exotic vodka cocktail.

mushrooms baked in vine leaves

farmhouse cheese with pomegranate and radicchio

2 tablespoons oil
1 tablespoon brown mustard seeds
1 teaspoon ground roast cumin
1 red capsicum (pepper), finely julienned
1 yellow capsicum (pepper), finely julienned
1 teaspoon sugar
1 small radicchio, leaves washed
200 g (7 oz) fresh farmhouse cheese or goat's curd
1 pomegranate, seeds separated out and juice reserved

Heat the oil in a large frying pan over a high heat and add the mustard seeds and ground cumin. As the seeds begin to pop, quickly add the capsicum and sugar. Toss until the capsicum is beginning to soften and then remove the pan from the heat.

To serve, make a bed of the radicchio leaves on a plate and top them with the capsicum. Add a scoop of the cheese and the pomegranate seeds before drizzling with any pomegranate juice. Season well. Serves 4

mushrooms baked in vine leaves

24–30 vine leaves in brine
4 large field mushrooms, stalks removed
12 cherry tomatoes
2 red onions, cut into eighths
4 sprigs thyme
4 tablespoons extra virgin olive oil
goat's cheese
fresh pesto (basics)

Preheat the oven to 180°C (350°F/Gas 4). Rinse the vine leaves and allow them to drain in a colander. Lay out four pieces of baking paper, each approximately 20 cm (8 in) square. Lay three large vine leaves at the centre of every square, overlapping the leaves to make a base. Sit one of the field mushrooms in the middle of each, cap-side-down.

Divide the cherry tomatoes, onion and thyme between the four mushrooms, piling them up in the cap. Pour over a little olive oil and cover the mushrooms with another three vine leaves, tucking the edges under to make a parcel. Draw in the four corners of each baking paper square so that they meet, then twist the joined corners to fasten the edges and seal in the vegetables. Put the four parcels onto a baking tray and bake for 1 1/2 hours.

To serve, remove the baking paper and the top leaves, so that the roast vegetables are sitting on a bed of baked vine leaves. Serve with olives, crusty bread and some crumbled goat's cheese and pesto. Serves 4

wild mushroom spaghetti

10 g (1/4 oz) dried porcini mushrooms
3 tablespoons olive oil
2 garlic cloves, chopped
1 onion, finely diced
2 field mushrooms, finely sliced
100 g (3 1/2 oz) fresh shiitake mushrooms, sliced
1/2 teaspoon thyme leaves
6 tablespoons white wine
100 g (3 1/2 oz) enoki mushrooms
400 g (14 oz) spaghetti
75 g (3/4 cup) finely grated Parmesan cheese

Bring a large pan of water to the boil for the pasta. Soak the dried mushrooms in 250 ml (1 cup) of boiling water for 15 minutes.

Heat the olive oil and fry the garlic and onions over a medium heat until they are soft and golden. Drain the mushrooms, straining the soaking liquid into a jug. Roughly slice the soaked mushrooms and add them to the onions, together with the field mushrooms, shiitake mushrooms and thyme. Cook them until the field mushrooms are soft and then add the white wine, mushroom soaking liquid and the enoki mushrooms. Season and reduce the heat to a low simmer.

Cook the pasta until *al dente*, then drain and return it to the warm pot. Add the Parmesan and stir through before dividing the pasta between four bowls. Top with the wild mushroom sauce. Serves 4

warm roast beef salad

4 Roma (plum) tomatoes, cut into quarters lengthways
125 ml (1/2 cup) oil
1 large eggplant (aubergine), finely sliced
450 g (1 lb) piece beef fillet
240 g (2 bunches) rocket (arugula)
4 tablespoons fresh pesto (basics)

Preheat the oven to 180°C (350°F/Gas 4). Put the tomatoes on a baking tray and season them with salt, pepper and a little white sugar before putting them in the oven for about 20 minutes.

Heat the oil in a frying pan over a high heat and fry the eggplant slices until they are lightly browned on both sides. Remove the eggplant and drain on paper towels. Pour away most of the oil and return the pan to a high heat.

Sear the beef fillet all over in the pan before putting it onto a baking tray and into the oven for 10 minutes (it will be rare at this point, so cook it for another 5 minutes if you prefer). Season the beef with salt, cover it with foil and let it rest for a few minutes.

Arrange the warm tomatoes and eggplant on a bed of rocket leaves. Finely slice the beef, arrange it on the salad and season well. Finish with a spoonful of pesto on top of the beef. Serves 4

roast beetroot salad

4 large beetroot
2 Lebanese (small) cucumbers, julienned
1/2 red onion, finely diced
2 tablespoons finely chopped dill
125 ml (1/2 cup) light sour cream
2 tablespoons grated fresh horseradish
1 tablespoon lemon juice
400 g (1 bunch) watercress, broken into sprigs

Preheat the oven to 180°C (350°F/Gas 4). Put the unpeeled beetroot into a roasting tin with 250 ml (1 cup) of water. Cover the tin with foil and bake for 1 hour or until a knife will pass easily through the beetroot. Remove the beetroot and allow them to cool.

Put the cucumber into a small bowl with the onion and fresh dill and mix them together. In a separate bowl, combine the sour cream with the horseradish and lemon juice and season to taste. Peel the skins from the beetroot — they should simply slip free, but it is a good idea to wear rubber gloves while doing this in case you need to rub the skins off. Cut the beetroot into thin slices.

Arrange the beetroot on a serving platter. Top with the cucumber salad and watercress, gently pour over the horseradish dressing, then season and serve. Serves 4 as a side dish

roast capsicum and green olive salad

2 red capsicums (peppers)
2 green capsicums (peppers)
2 yellow capsicums (peppers)
2 garlic cloves, peeled and finely chopped
75 g (1/2 bunch) parsley, roughly chopped
10 large basil leaves, roughly chopped
12 green olives, pitted and sliced
3 tablespoons olive oil
1 tablespoon balsamic vinegar

Roast the capsicums whole in a hot oven — 200°C (400°F/Gas 6) — or over a gas flame until the skin blisters, then put them in a plastic bag or covered bowl and allow them to cool. Seed and skin the capsicums, then finely slice them and put them in a bowl together with the garlic, parsley, sliced green olives, olive oil and balsamic vinegar.

Toss the salad ingredients to combine and season according to taste. Serves 6 as a side dish

coconut and green bean salad

warm leek salad

coconut and green bean salad

400 g (14 oz) green beans
2 green chillies, finely chopped
1 teaspoon grated fresh ginger
80 ml (1/3 cup) plain yoghurt
1 lime, juiced
1 teaspoon sea salt
1/4 coconut, flesh freshly shaved
2 tablespoons vegetable oil
1 tablespoon brown mustard seeds
30 curry leaves

Bring a saucepan of water to the boil and cook the green beans for 2 to 3 minutes until they are brilliant green. Drain and refresh the beans under running cold water.

Put the chillies, ginger, yoghurt, lime juice and sea salt in a bowl, add the coconut and toss everything together.

Heat the oil over a medium heat in a small frying pan, add the mustard seeds and curry leaves, and when the seeds begin to pop take the pan off the heat. Add the seeds and leaves to the coconut mixture with the green beans and toss them together. Serves 4 as a side dish

white bean salad

2 tablespoons olive oil
2 garlic cloves, crushed
1 red onion, cut into wedges
50 g (1 bunch) thyme, broken into sprigs
60 ml (1/4 cup) white wine
1 x 400 g (14 oz) tin cannellini beans
150 g (1 punnet) cherry tomatoes, halved
1 tablespoon balsamic vinegar
30 g (1 cup) roughly chopped flat-leaf (Italian) parsley

Heat the oil in a frying pan over a medium heat. Add the garlic and cook until lightly golden before adding the red onion and thyme. Continue cooking until the onion is soft and transparent, then pour in the white wine. Simmer until the wine has reduced to almost nothing before mixing in the beans. Stir to combine and then remove the bean mixture from the heat.

Tip the beans into a bowl, add the tomatoes, vinegar and parsley, stir to combine and season to taste. You may also wish to add a little virgin olive oil to give the salad a rich gloss. Serves 4 as a side dish

warm leek salad

1 generous pinch saffron
3 tablespoons butter
125 ml (1/2 cup) white wine
24 baby leeks
4 slices prosciutto
1 tablespoon olive oil
12 sage leaves
16 Niçoise olives
70 g (2 1/2 oz) creamy blue cheese
1 tablespoon small capers

Preheat the oven to 180°C (350°F/Gas 4). Put a deep roasting tin over a high heat and sprinkle in the saffron, letting it heat through before adding the butter. As it sizzles, add the wine and leeks. Take the tin off the heat, cover with foil and bake for 40 minutes.

Meanwhile, heat a frying pan and cook the prosciutto until it is crisp and golden, draining it on paper towels. Add the olive oil to the pan and fry the sage leaves. When they are beginning to crisp up, remove them and drain them on paper towels. Toss the olives in the hot oil and then remove the pan from the heat, leaving the olives in the pan.

When the leeks are cooked, arrange them on four warmed plates. Top the vegetables with the prosciutto, cheese, capers, sage leaves and olives, then pour over some of the juices from the frying pan and the roasting tin. Serves 4 as a starter

fresh and fast

- The easiest way to open a whole coconut is to put it in a hot oven for 5 to 10 minutes and allow the heat to partially crack the shell.

- Use a vegetable peeler to shave thin slices of fresh coconut into a salad of snow peas (mangetout), finely sliced spring onion (scallion) and capsicum (pepper). Drizzle with a sweet mirin and ginger dressing and serve with grilled chicken.

- Use the recipe for the yoghurt dressing on the coconut and green bean salad to marinate chicken breasts. Bake them and serve with mango pickle.

- The saffron leeks make a flavourful side dish for grilled chicken or fish. Slice the leeks into smaller pieces and add a squeeze of lemon juice if serving with fish, a scattering of parsley and oregano leaves if it is accompanying chicken.

white bean salad

swordfish with prosciutto

baked salmon with hijiki and radish salad

swordfish with prosciutto

8 Kalamata olives, pitted
3 tablespoons butter, softened
2 tablespoons light olive oil
4 slices prosciutto
400 g (14 oz) kipfler or salad potatoes, finely sliced
6 spring onions (scallions), trimmed and sliced on the diagonal
375 ml (1 1/2 cups) white wine
4 x 200 g (7 oz) swordfish steaks

Finely chop the olives and stir them into the butter. Heat the oil in a large frying pan over a medium heat, add the prosciutto and fry until crisp. Once the prosciutto is cooked, move it to the side of the pan and put in the potatoes and spring onions. When the potatoes begin to soften, add the white wine and the swordfish steaks, arranging the swordfish on top of the potatoes and putting a piece of cooked prosciutto on top of each steak. Cover the pan and simmer for 12 minutes.

Check that the fish is cooked through and then serve the swordfish and potatoes on warmed serving plates. Divide the olive butter between the steaks and spoon the wine sauce over the top. Serve with a green salad or steamed green beans.
Serves 4

salad of roast potatoes and smoked trout

4 large potatoes, cut into wedges
1 lemon, zested and juiced
125 ml (1/2 cup) light olive oil
2 tablespoons finely chopped dill
400 g (14 oz) hot smoked ocean trout, broken into pieces
100 g (3 handfuls) baby spinach leaves
15 g (1/2 cup) roughly chopped flat-leaf (Italian) parsley

Preheat the oven to 180°C (350°F/Gas 4). Put the potatoes in a baking dish with 250 ml (1 cup) of water, season generously with sea salt and add the lemon zest and 4 tablespoons of oil. Bake for 20 minutes.

Meanwhile, whisk the lemon juice with the oil and dill. Season to taste.

Turn the potatoes over and cook them for a further 20 minutes. When the potatoes are golden brown, divide them between four plates. Top with the ocean trout, spinach leaves and a scattering of parsley. Spoon the dill dressing over the salad just before serving. Serves 4

baked salmon with hijiki and radish salad

2 tablespoons hijiki
6 umeboshi plums, seeds removed
4 tablespoons mirin
2 teaspoons sesame oil
4 x 200 g (7 oz) salmon fillets, skin on
2 tablespoons oil
300 g (10 1/2 oz) daikon, julienned
1 tablespoon finely sliced pickled ginger
1 tablespoon pickled ginger juice
400 g (1 bunch) watercress, leaves only

Preheat the oven to 180°C (350°F/Gas 4). Soak the hijiki in warm water for about 20 minutes. Mash the plums until they are soft and then combine them with the mirin and sesame oil.

Rinse the salmon fillets in cold water and pat them dry with paper towels. Rub the plum glaze into the flesh of the fish.

Heat the oil in a frying pan with an ovenproof handle over a high heat and add the salmon fillets skin-side-down. Sear the fish for a few minutes and then put the pan in the oven to bake for 10 minutes.

Meanwhile toss the hijiki, daikon, ginger and ginger juice together in a bowl with the watercress leaves. Pile the mixture onto four plates and top with the salmon fillet. Serves 4

fresh and fast

• Add finely shredded daikon to noodle salads or toss it with sliced snow peas (mangetout), soy sauce and sesame seeds for a grilled fish accompaniment.

• Daikon becomes sweet with slow cooking and makes a great cool-weather addition to duck or slippery noodles. Simmer thick chunks of daikon in a vegetable or dashi broth with fresh ginger and garlic chives. Add shiitake mushrooms to enrich the flavour, or add chilli and rounds of leek to give depth.

• Make a great base for any warming pasta sauce by sautéing several finely sliced leeks and a little prosciutto together. Add your favourite flavours — perhaps tomato and olive, fresh parsley and tuna or ricotta and Parmesan cheese.

• Hot-smoked fish is beginning to make an appearance in most supermarket aisles and makes a wonderful stand-by ingredient which can be added to pasta dishes, broken into salads or simply served whole with warm greens and boiled new potatoes.

salad of roast potatoes and smoked trout

spiced potatoes

4 tablespoons olive oil
500 g (1 lb 2 oz) potatoes, peeled and diced
2 large red chillies, seeded and finely chopped
3 garlic cloves, crushed
1 teaspoon ground cumin
1/2 teaspoon ground coriander
1/2 teaspoon paprika
lime wedges
2 tablespoons lime juice
20 g (1 cup) fresh coriander (cilantro) leaves

Heat the olive oil in a heavy-based frying pan over a medium heat. Add the potatoes to the oil and stir them so that they are all well coated. Add the chillies, garlic, spices and some salt.

Stir the potatoes carefully around the pan until they are soft and golden. Put them on a serving platter with lime wedges, spoon the lime juice over the potatoes and garnish with the coriander leaves. Serves 4 as a side dish

honeyed duck breast with chinese cabbage

4 duck breasts
1 teaspoon Chinese five-spice powder
1 teaspoon salt
2 tablespoons butter
500 g (1 lb 2 oz) Chinese cabbage, finely sliced
2 tablespoons honey
2 oranges, juiced

Preheat the oven to 200°C (400°F/Gas 6). Score the skin of the duck breasts in a criss-cross pattern and rub the five-spice powder into the skin along with some salt.

Melt the butter in a frying pan over a moderate heat, add the cabbage, then sauté for several minutes until the cabbage is soft and slightly transparent. Season and reduce the heat to low.

Drizzle the honey over the duck breasts and put them into the preheated oven for 15 minutes. Check that the breasts are cooked through, allow them to rest for a minute covered with foil and then slice them thinly.

Serve the duck with the cabbage and a drizzle of fresh orange juice. Serves 4

warm salad of fennel and salami

340 g (12 oz) small fennel bulbs
10 sprigs thyme
4 tablespoons extra virgin olive oil
2 tablespoons balsamic vinegar
16 slices spicy salami
120 g (1 bunch) rocket (arugula)
150 g (1 cup) crumbled creamy Persian feta cheese

Preheat the oven to 180°C (350°F/Gas 4). Slice the fennel bulbs lengthways into quarters or eighths depending on how big they are and put them on a baking tray. Add the thyme and olive oil. Toss everything together, season and then cover with foil and bake for half an hour.

When the fennel has cooked through, drizzle it with the balsamic vinegar. Lay the salami slices on a baking tray and put them under the grill for 2 to 3 minutes or until they are slightly crisp. Arrange the rocket on four plates and top with the warm fennel, the crisp salami and some crumbled feta. Serves 4

capsicum and potato stew with saffron

2 tablespoons butter
2 red onions, peeled and diced
2 garlic cloves, crushed
1 large pinch saffron threads
1 x 400 g (14 oz) tin chopped tomatoes
1 teaspoon sugar
700 g (1 lb 9 oz) waxy potatoes, cut into bite-size pieces
1 red capsicum (pepper), cut into thick strips
1 teaspoon thyme leaves
15 g (1/2 cup) coriander (cilantro) leaves
30 g (1 bunch) chives, finely chopped

Heat the butter, onions, garlic and saffron together in a large saucepan over a medium heat. When the onion is soft and transparent, add the tomatoes, sugar and 500 ml (2 cups) of water. Cover with a lid and simmer for 10 minutes.

Add the potatoes to the tomato along with the capsicum and thyme, then cover and simmer for a further 35 minutes. Season to taste with sea salt and freshly ground black pepper and serve sprinkled with the coriander and chives. Serves 4 as a side dish

fillet steak with an onion and mushroom sauce

Use one — or a selection — of the different kinds of mushrooms available now to add depth of flavour and texture to a dish.

fillet steak with an onion and mushroom sauce

10 g (2 tablespoons) dried porcini mushrooms
2 red onions, cut into eighths lengthways
250 ml (1 cup) red wine
1 garlic clove, crushed
1 tablespoon olive oil
4 x 175 g (6 oz) fillet steaks
100 g (3 1/2 oz) oyster mushrooms
2 tablespoons butter
borlotti bean and chopped basil salad

Soak the dried mushrooms in 250 ml (1 cup) of boiling water, then drain, reserving the liquid. Put the onions in a large saucepan and add the wine, garlic and the mushroom soaking liquid. Slice the soaked mushrooms finely and add them to the saucepan. Bring everything to the boil, then reduce the heat to a low simmer and cook for 30 minutes or until the liquid has almost evaporated.

Heat a heavy-based frying pan over a high heat and add the oil. As it begins to smoke, add the steaks and sear them until the uncooked surface looks slightly bloody. Turn each steak over and cook for a further minute before taking the pan off the heat. Season the steaks and let them sit for a few minutes in the pan.

Add the oyster mushrooms and butter to the onion mix and cook for another minute. Serve the steaks on warmed plates with a salad of borlotti beans and chopped basil, and spoon the onion sauce over the steaks. Serves 4

spiced duck breast

4 duck breast fillets, skin on
2 tablespoons brown sugar
1/2 teaspoon Sichuan peppercorns
1 star anise
1 tablespoon sea salt
125 ml (1/2 cup) brandy
4 dried shiitake mushrooms
2 thin leeks, cut into lengths
400 g (14 oz) Jap or butternut pumpkin (squash), cubed
2 tablespoons light olive oil

Preheat the oven to 180°C (350°F/Gas 4). Score the skin of the duck in a criss-cross pattern. Put the brown sugar, peppercorns and star anise into a spice grinder or mortar and pestle with the sea salt and grind them together. Rub this mixture into the duck skin. Put the brandy in a small container, add the duck breasts, skin-side-up, cover and marinate for at least an hour or overnight.

Soak the dried mushrooms in 500 ml (2 cups) of boiling water for half an hour, then strain the liquid into a baking dish and finely slice the mushrooms. Put the mushroom slices in the baking dish with the leeks and pumpkin, season, cover with foil and bake for 30 minutes until the pumpkin is soft. Turn the oven up to 200°C (400°F/Gas 6).

Heat a frying pan over a high heat and sear the duck, skin-side-down, until it is lightly browned. Put the duck breasts onto a rack set over a baking tray, this time skin-side-up, and drizzle them with the brandy marinade. Roast them for 15 minutes. (If the duck skin hasn't completely crisped up in your oven, place the skin under a hot grill for a minute.) Arrange the pumpkin and leek on four warmed plates and top with a thinly sliced duck breast. Serves 4

caramelized fennel and apple

1 tablespoon butter
1 small fennel bulb, finely sliced
20 sage leaves
2 green apples, cored and finely sliced
3 tablespoons white wine
1 teaspoon sugar

Melt the butter in a large heavy-based pan over a medium heat and add the fennel. Sauté the fennel until it is golden and soft, then add the sage leaves and cook for a minute. Season with sea salt and white pepper before adding the apple, white wine and sugar.

Cover and cook for a few minutes until the apples are just beginning to soften and caramelize. Be careful not to let them get too dark. Serve with grilled pork chops or roast pork loin. Serves 4 as a side dish

sichuan eggplant

250 ml (1 cup) oil
2 small eggplants (aubergines), cut into pieces
2 large red chillies, seeded and finely sliced
1 teaspoon roasted Sichuan peppercorns, ground
2 garlic cloves, finely chopped
1 1/2 tablespoons finely grated fresh ginger
4 spring onions (scallions), sliced diagonally
60 ml (1/4 cup) light soy sauce
1 tablespoon balsamic vinegar
1 teaspoon sugar

Heat the oil in a wok or deep saucepan and deep-fry the eggplant in batches until it is golden brown. Take the eggplant out using a slotted spoon and drain it on paper towels. Pour most of the oil out of the wok, leaving behind about a tablespoon.

Reheat the oil and add the chilli, peppercorns, garlic, ginger and spring onions. Stir-fry for 30 seconds, put in the fried eggplant, soy sauce, vinegar and sugar and stir-fry for another minute. Serve on a bed of buckwheat or somen noodles. Serves 4 as a starter

spice-crusted fish

2 tablespoons coriander seeds
2 tablespoons cumin seeds
1 1/2 tablespoons sea salt
1 garlic clove
40 g (2 cups) flat-leaf (Italian) parsley leaves
2 tablespoons extra virgin olive oil
4 x 200 g (7 oz) blue-eye cod or white fish fillets
2 tablespoons light olive oil
mashed potato
lemon wedges

Preheat the oven to 180°C (350°F/Gas 4). Put the coriander and cumin seeds on a tray and roast them in the oven for 2 minutes until they begin to darken. Remove, cool briefly and put them in a mortar and pestle or spice grinder with the salt and a generous amount of black pepper. Grind to a powder, then add the garlic, parsley and extra virgin olive oil. Work the seasoning to a thick paste. Rinse the cod in cold water and pat dry with paper towels. Pat the paste onto the top of each of the fish fillets, forming a thickish crust that completely covers the surface.

Heat the light oil in a large ovenproof frying pan over a high heat until it begins to shimmer. Add the fish to the pan, crust-side-down. Sear for a minute, turn it over and cook for another minute. Put the pan in the oven for 5 minutes. Remove the fish and serve on a bed of mashed potato with lemon wedges. Serves 4

warm salad of chestnuts and brussels sprouts

200 g (7 oz) fresh chestnuts
300 g (10 1/2 oz) Brussels sprouts, trimmed and cut in half
4 tablespoons butter
1 tablespoon lemon juice
2 tablespoons roughly chopped parsley

Preheat the oven to 200°C (400°F/Gas 6). Cut a gash in the outer shell of each of the chestnuts, put them on a baking tray and roast them for 15 to 20 minutes or until the shells split. Peel the chestnuts while they are still warm and rub off their inner skins. Any particularly stubborn ones can be boiled for a couple of minutes to loosen them. Cut them in half if you like.

Bring a saucepan of water to the boil, tip in the Brussels sprouts and cook them for 5 minutes. When the sprouts are ready, heat the butter in a frying pan over a high heat until it begins to turn a golden brown colour. Add the lemon juice, chestnuts and Brussels sprouts to the pan and toss them together. Season to taste and at the last moment scatter over the chopped parsley. Serves 4

creamed rice with vanilla-glazed oranges

vanilla panna cotta with toffee apples

creamed rice with vanilla-glazed oranges

110 g (1/2 cup) short grain rice
500 ml (2 cups) milk
1 vanilla pod, split
4 strips lemon zest
4 tablespoons sugar
125 ml (1/2 cup) cream, whipped
vanilla-glazed oranges (basics)

Preheat the oven to 180°C (350°F/Gas 4). Rinse the rice in cold water and drain it. Bring the milk to the boil with the vanilla pod, lemon zest and the sugar, add the rice and simmer gently for 30 minutes, stirring occasionally.

When the rice has cooked, allow it to cool a little and then fold in the whipped cream. Spoon the rice into bowls and serve with the vanilla-glazed oranges. Serves 6

jaffa mousse

140 g (5 oz) bitter chocolate
4 tablespoons Grand Marnier
4 egg yolks
4 tablespoons cocoa
2 teaspoons grated orange zest
185 ml (3/4 cup) cream, whipped
4 oranges

Melt the chocolate and 2 tablespoons of Grand Marnier in a bowl set over a saucepan of simmering water. Add the egg yolks, one at a time, stirring each one well into the chocolate mixture before adding the next. The chocolate may begin to stiffen but it will soon become smooth again. When you have added all the yolks, take the chocolate mixture off the heat and cool it a little.

Fold the cocoa and grated orange zest into the whipped cream, then fold the cream into the chocolate. Pour the mixture into a bowl and leave it in the fridge for several hours to chill.

Peel the oranges with a sharp knife and cut them into slices. Put the orange slices in a bowl with 2 tablespoons of Grand Marnier. Divide the oranges between four to six dessert plates and top with a large spoonful of the mousse. Serves 4–6

vanilla panna cotta with toffee apples

875 ml (3 1/2 cups) cream
2 lemons, zest finely grated, juiced
115 g (1/2 cup) caster (superfine) sugar
2 vanilla beans, halved lengthways
3 gelatine leaves
toffee apples (basics)

Whip 250 ml (1 cup) of cream and put it in the fridge. Put the remaining cream, lemon zest and juice, sugar and vanilla in a saucepan and heat gently over a low heat to melt the sugar. Do not let it boil.

Take the pan off the heat and, using the end of a sharp knife, scrape the seeds from the inside of each of the vanilla pods into the cream mixture (you can keep the pods for later use). Soak the gelatine sheets in a bowl of cold water. When the sheets are soft, squeeze out any excess water and stir them into the warm cream.

Allow the vanilla cream to cool before lightly folding through the whipped cream. Pour the mixture into eight tea cups or moulds, cover them with plastic wrap and chill in the fridge for 3 hours or overnight. The panna cottas can be served in their cups with the apples on the side, or you can turn them out by dipping the base of each of the moulds briefly into a bowl of hot water and upending them onto the plate. Give them a little shake to loosen them. Serve with warm toffee apples. Serves 8

fresh and fast

• Slow-bake thin slices of quince with sugar, orange juice and some freshly grated ginger. Serve the quince piled over chocolate brownies with a dollop of cream.

• The richness of quince is perfectly suited to fresh cheeses such as ricotta. Serve thin slices of quince or quince paste with ricotta and thin crackers for a dessert that isn't overly sweet.

• For a winter fruit salad, use a sharp knife to remove orange segments from 4 to 6 oranges. Squeeze the remaining flesh of the orange to release any excess juice. Add thin slices of banana and red apple, the juice of 1 lemon and brown sugar to taste. Serve with vanilla ice cream or creamy yoghurt.

jaffa mousse

The beurre bosc pear is not only ideal for slow cooking, its delicately flavoured flesh is also perfect for slicing into peppery salads. 151

baked figs with pistachios

pear and ginger cake

2 tablespoons unsalted butter
55 g (1/2 cup) ground almonds
3 eggs
125 ml (1/2 cup) milk
400 g (1 3/4 cups) caster (superfine) sugar
1 tablespoon grated fresh ginger
250 g (2 cups) plain (all-purpose) flour
2 teaspoons baking powder
3–5 beurre bosc pears, cored and sliced lengthways
icing (powdered) sugar

Preheat the oven to 180°C (350°F/Gas 4). Butter a round 20 cm (8 in) springform cake tin with 1 tablespoon of butter. Sprinkle in half of the ground almonds and shake them around so that they stick to the buttered cake tin.

Put the eggs, milk, sugar, ginger, flour and baking powder into a food processor or large bowl and process or mix to make a thick batter. Fold the pears into the batter and then spoon the mixture into the cake tin. Sprinkle the top of the batter with the remaining ground almonds and dot with the rest of the butter.

Bake for 1 1/2 hours, check to see if it is cooked through, remove and cool. Dust with icing sugar and serve with whipped cream. Serves 8

baked figs with pistachios

4 large figs
4 teaspoons brown sugar
1 orange, zested and juiced
1 tablespoon unsalted butter
50 g (1/3 cup) shelled unsalted pistachio nuts
1/2 teaspoon ground cinnamon
1 tablespoon honey
250 g (1 cup) mascarpone cheese

Preheat the oven to 180°C (350°F/Gas 4). Slice the figs into quarters lengthways from the top downwards, being careful not to slice all the way through. Sit them in a baking dish and put a heaped teaspoon of brown sugar and some of the orange zest into the centre of each fig. Divide the butter between the figs and dot it on top of the sugar. Add the pistachios and orange juice to the dish and sprinkle with a little cinnamon. Bake the figs for 10 minutes.

Meanwhile, blend the honey into the mascarpone until it has a smooth consistency.

To serve, carefully remove the figs from the dish and put a spoonful of honeyed mascarpone in the middle of each. Spoon over the juice and pistachios and serve while still warm. Serves 4

baked quinces with orange and cardamom almond bread

berry chocolate tart

baked quinces with orange and cardamom almond bread

2 large quinces, peeled, cored and quartered
2 oranges, juiced
3 tablespoons sugar
2 tablespoons honey
cardamom almond bread (basics)
icing (powdered) sugar
plain yoghurt or thick (double/heavy) cream

Preheat the oven to 180°C (350°F/Gas 4). Line a baking tray with baking paper and lay the quince pieces on it. Cover them with the orange juice, sugar and honey and another piece of baking paper and put them in the oven.

After an hour, reduce the oven heat to 140°C (275°F/Gas 1) and bake the quinces for a further 2 hours or until they are soft and have turned a deep ruby red.

Serve the quinces with the almond bread dusted with icing sugar, and with yoghurt or thick cream. Serves 4

berry chocolate tart

4 teaspoons strawberry jam
1 prebaked chocolate tart case (basics)
160 g (5 1/2 oz) unsalted butter
200 g (7 oz) dark chocolate
3 egg yolks
2 eggs
4 tablespoons caster (superfine) sugar
2 tablespoons Grand Marnier
cocoa
fresh berries

Preheat the oven to 180°C (350°F/Gas 4). Spoon the jam onto the base of the tart case and put it into the oven for 2 minutes. Remove the tart case and use a pastry brush to brush the warm jam gently over the base until it is glazed all over.

Melt the butter and chocolate together in a saucepan over a very low heat. Beat the yolks, eggs and sugar until they are light and fluffy. Pour the melted chocolate and Grand Marnier into the eggs and continue to beat for a minute.

Pour the chocolate filling into the tart case and return it to the oven for 5 minutes. Allow it to sit for at least 2 hours before serving it, dusted with cocoa, with a pile of fresh berries. Serves 8

fig and burnt butter tart

6 figs
1 prebaked shortcrust tart case (basics)
3 eggs
170 g (3/4 cup) caster (superfine) sugar
3 tablespoons plain (all-purpose) flour
185 g (6 1/2 oz) unsalted butter

Preheat the oven to 180°C (350°F/Gas 4). Slice the figs into quarters and arrange them in the prebaked tart case with the narrow ends pointing up.

Beat the eggs and sugar until they are pale and fluffy and fold in the flour. Heat the butter in a saucepan over a high heat, and when it begins to froth and turn a biscuit colour pour the hot butter into the egg mixture and continue to beat for a minute. Pour the filling over the figs and bake for 25 minutes or until the filling is cooked and golden brown.

Allow the tart to cool before serving. Serves 8

fresh and fast

- Sprinkle finely sliced oranges with cinnamon and serve with honey-laced mascarpone cheese and brandy snap biscuits.

- Make a simple apple pudding. Put peeled and cored wedges of green apple into a baking dish. Rub enough unsalted butter into 160 g (2 cups) of breadcrumbs to make them slightly sticky. Sprinkle the breadcrumbs over the apple, drizzle with golden syrup and bake for half an hour or until the breadcrumbs are golden brown. Serve with ice cream and another spoonful of golden syrup.

- Marinate quarters of fig in Grand Marnier or your favourite liqueur and serve with a scoop of vanilla bean ice cream.

- Serve a selection of figs, pears and purple grapes with cheeses such as creamy rich dolcelatte or a runny Brie. Accompany with some seeded lavash or crisp crackers and a good dessert wine, then sit back and enjoy.

fig and burnt butter tart

winter

Winter is when the big pots come out. Don't panic, we're not talking about spending hours in the kitchen — although, sometimes, standing by a hot stove is exactly where you want to find yourself on a blustery grey day. Rather, this is the season for slow food. The kind of food that you throw into a heavy casserole dish and then forget for a couple of hours, allowing the combination of heat and great produce to work its alchemy with very little interference from you. Just lift the lid, then gather with friends around a pot of rich velvety meat or hearty vegetables. This kind of food needs little more than a side dish of creamy mash or spicy couscous to turn it into the culinary equivalent of a soft, thick blanket. So set the oven timer, add some drama to the table using dark, luscious colours, curl up with a warming red wine and enjoy the best that winter has to offer.

potatoes

brussels sprouts

turnips

shallots

parsnips

kale

horseradish

garlic

cabbages

carrots

broccoli

brown onions

chestnuts

apples

lemons

pears

rhubarb

grapefruit

good ideas

winter greens

'Good for you' greens don't have to be boring. Drizzle them with herb-infused olive oil, some savoury–sweet kecap manis, lime juice and chilli flakes, oyster sauce, toasted sesame seeds, butter and mustard or a scattering of warm pine nuts.

garlic

Put several whole heads of garlic in a baking dish with some olive oil and a little rosemary. Cover and bake until the garlic is soft. Remove the roasted flesh, purée it with the rosemary oil and serve on toasted bread, topped with some fresh parsley or thinly sliced Parmesan cheese.

apples

The easiest apple tart in the world is made from melting together 100 g (3^{1}/$_{2}$ oz) unsalted butter and 110 g (^{1}/$_{2}$ cup) sugar. Add 1 teaspoon cinnamon, 2 grated green apples, 1 teaspoon lemon juice and 2 eggs. Fold them together, pour into a prebaked tart case and bake for 30 minutes or until golden brown. Or simpler still, cut out rounds of butter puff pastry and put them on a baking tray. Top with finely sliced green apple, a sprinkle of sugar and a dab of butter. Bake until golden.

rhubarb

Simmer rhubarb stalks with enough sugar to cut their tartness and then serve with cinnamon toast. For a luscious dessert, put roughly chopped stalks in a covered ovenproof dish and bake with brown sugar, orange juice, orange zest and a split vanilla pod.

parsnips

Sticky with pan juices and sweet at the centre, a roast parsnip is a wonderful thing. Always add parsnips to your selection of roast vegetables or combine them in a pot with potatoes for a fragrant mash that will blend perfectly with grilled sausages.

potatoes

The most important thing to remember when buying potatoes is that different potatoes suit different purposes. Ask your greengrocer which potatoes are best suited to salads, roasting or mashing and start to experiment with some of the newer varieties. For a quick meal that rates high on the comfort barometer, fry some chopped bacon in a pan with butter until crisp, then add small chunks of boiled potato, a few handfuls of spinach, some parsley and a drizzle of olive oil. Cook until the spinach has just wilted, season and pile into warm bowls.

tomato and cheese tartlets

leek and lemon fettucine

tomato and cheese tartlets

8 Roma (plum) tomatoes, cut into eighths
250 ml (1 cup) thick (double/heavy) cream
3 eggs
150 g (1 cup) grated Gruyère cheese
150 g (1 1/2 cups) grated Parmesan cheese
6 prebaked 8 cm (3 in) tartlet cases (basics)
2 tablespoons oregano leaves
18 basil leaves, roughly torn
1 tablespoon extra virgin olive oil

Preheat the oven to 180°C (350°F/Gas 4). Put the tomatoes on a baking tray, sprinkle them with salt and pepper and bake them in the oven for half an hour.

Whisk together the cream, eggs, Gruyère and Parmesan and pour the mixture into the six tartlet cases. Bake for 20 minutes or until the eggs are set and the filling is golden brown.

Put the tomatoes in a small bowl with the oregano, basil and olive oil, toss them together and then pile some tomatoes on top of each tartlet. Serve as is or on a bed of leafy greens. Makes 6

leek and lemon fettucine

3 tablespoons olive oil
3 garlic cloves, crushed
1 tablespoon fresh oregano leaves
3 large leeks, finely sliced
400 g (14 oz) fettucine
1 lemon, zest grated
1 tablespoon small capers
70 g (2/3 cup) grated Parmesan cheese
30 g (1 cup) roughly chopped flat-leaf (Italian) parsley
grated Parmesan cheese

Bring a large saucepan of water to the boil for the pasta. Heat the olive oil in a large frying pan over a medium heat and then add the minced garlic, oregano and leeks. Sauté until the leeks are soft and transparent, then season with sea salt and freshly ground black pepper.

Cook the pasta until it is *al dente*, then drain and return it to the warm pan. Add the leeks, grated lemon zest, capers, Parmesan and parsley, stirring them into the pasta. Season, then serve with extra Parmesan. Serves 4

seared snapper with spiced butter

4 tablespoons butter, softened
1 onion, finely diced
1 tablespoon brown mustard seeds
1 teaspoon cayenne pepper
1 teaspoon curry powder
7 g (1/4 cup) finely chopped coriander (cilantro) leaves
4 x 175 g (6 oz) snapper fillets
1 tablespoon vegetable oil
steamed green beans
lime wedges
leaf salad

Put 1 tablespoon of butter in a frying pan over a medium heat and add the diced onion. Sauté until the onion is soft and lightly golden, then add the mustard seeds, cayenne pepper and curry powder and cook for a further couple of minutes. Remove from the heat and set aside to cool. When the onion mixture has cooled, fold in the remaining butter and chopped coriander.

Rinse the snapper fillets in cold water and pat them dry with some paper towels. Heat the oil in a frying pan over a high heat and add the snapper fillets, skin-side-down. Fry for several minutes until the skin is lightly browned, then flip the fish over and cook the other side for a further 2 to 3 minutes depending on the thickness of the fillet. Serve on a bed of green beans with the spiced butter, some lime wedges and a leaf salad. Serves 4

fresh and fast

- Using a deep-based frying pan, fry several finely sliced onions in olive oil until they are soft and a little caramelized. Add some fresh oregano, parsley and finely chopped tomatoes, pour 6 beaten eggs over the vegetables and top with grated Gruyère cheese. Finish cooking the frittata under a hot grill, cut it into thick wedges and enjoy it with buttery toast.

- Lemon is always beautiful in pasta. For a quick and easy pasta dish, finely dice half a red onion. Add some olive oil, salt and pepper, a generous amount of roughly chopped parsley, olives, a few torn anchovies and lemon zest. Toss the warm pasta through the raw ingredients and serve with lots of grated Parmesan cheese.

- Flavoured butters are a great way to make a dish taste special with very little work. They can be made in advance and stored in the fridge. Try combinations like ginger and lime, lemon and caper or mixed herb.

seared snapper with spiced butter

white bean and green herb soup

2 tablespoons olive oil
2 onions, finely diced
200 g (2 cups) finely sliced celery
1 litre (4 cups) vegetable stock or chicken stock
400 g (1½ cups) cooked white beans such as cannellini
45 g (1½ cups) roughly chopped flat-leaf (Italian) parsley
10 basil leaves, finely chopped
125 ml (½ cup) light sour cream
10 mint leaves, finely chopped
crusty bread

Heat the oil in a large saucepan over a medium heat. Add the onions and celery and sauté until the onions are soft and transparent. Mix in the vegetable stock and white beans and simmer for half an hour.

Just before serving, add the parsley and basil. Cook for a further minute and then ladle the soup into four soup bowls. Add the sour cream, garnish with the chopped mint and serve with thick slices of crusty bread. Serves 4

lentil and fennel sausage salad

200 g (1 cup) Puy lentils
1 teaspoon sea salt
1 tablespoon balsamic vinegar
4 tablespoons extra virgin olive oil
1 tablespoon whole grain mustard
8 fennel sausages
½ red onion, finely sliced
50 g (1 cup) croutons (basics)
20 g (1 cup) parsley leaves

Put the lentils in a saucepan with 1 litre (4 cups) of water and the sea salt, bring to the boil, reduce the heat and simmer for half an hour. When the lentils are tender, drain them of any excess water and stir in the vinegar, 2 tablespoons of olive oil and the mustard.

Cook the sausages in a frying pan or under the grill until they are browned and cooked through.

At the last minute toss the red onion, croutons and parsley through the lentils, divide them between four plates and drizzle them with a little more olive oil. Top with the sausages and serve with a blob of extra mustard. Serves 4

steak with caramelized rosemary shallots

1 tablespoon butter
200 g (7 oz) baby onions or shallots,
    sliced in half if large
4 sprigs rosemary
1 teaspoon sugar
185 ml (¾ cup) red wine
1 teaspoon balsamic vinegar
1 teaspoon olive oil
4 x 200 g (7 oz) fillet steaks

Heat the butter in a saucepan over a medium heat and add the shallots. Toss the shallots around until they are golden and beginning to soften, then add the rosemary and cook until the shallots are caramelized on the outside. Add the sugar and swirl it around the pan until it has dissolved, before pouring in the red wine and balsamic vinegar. Allow the sauce to simmer for a couple of minutes to reduce the liquid by half.

Heat a heavy cast-iron frying pan over a high heat and add the olive oil. As it begins to smoke, add the steaks and sear them until the uncooked surface begins to look slightly bloody. Turn each of the steaks over and cook for a further minute. Season and allow the steak to rest for a few minutes in the pan. Spoon the shallots over and serve with a dollop of creamy mashed potato. Serves 4

barley risotto with wilted greens

2 tablespoons butter
2 garlic cloves, crushed
1 tablespoon thyme leaves
3 onions, finely sliced
220 g (1 cup) pearl barley
1 lemon, zest grated
1 litre (4 cups) chicken stock
70 g (⅔ cup) grated Parmesan cheese
1 tablespoon olive oil
900 g (2 bunches) kale or water spinach, roughly chopped
grated Parmesan cheese

Heat the butter in a large saucepan over a medium heat and add the garlic and thyme. When the garlic begins to soften, add the onions and cook until they are soft. Mix in the pearl barley and lemon zest and stir for a few minutes until the barley is well coated and glistening.

Add 250 ml (1 cup) of stock and simmer, stirring until the stock has been absorbed. Continue to add the stock a little at a time until it has all been taken up by the pearl barley. Just as the last of the stock has been absorbed, stir in the grated Parmesan. Meanwhile, heat a pan or wok over a high heat and add the olive oil. Toss in the kale and quickly stir-fry until the greens are just cooked. Spoon the risotto into four warmed bowls, and top with some of the greens. Serve with extra Parmesan. Serves 4

tomato and tofu broth

white chicken salad

4 spring onions (scallions), finely sliced, green tops reserved
1 stalk lemon grass, bruised
80 g (1 bunch) coriander (cilantro)
1 tablespoon sea salt
2 chicken breast fillets
400 g (2 cups) jasmine rice
90 g (1 bunch) mint
1 large red chilli, seeded and finely chopped
300 g (10$^{1}/_{2}$ oz) silken firm tofu, cut into 4 thick slices
soy sauce
lime wedges

Put the green tops of the spring onions into a large saucepan with the lemon grass and coriander roots and stalks. Fill the pan with water, add the salt and bring to the boil. Drop the chicken into the stock, cover the pan and remove it from the heat. Leave it covered for 40 minutes, then lift the fillets out of the stock and check that they are cooked. Finely slice them across the grain.

Put the rice and 685 ml (2$^{3}/_{4}$ cups) of the strained cooking liquid in a saucepan. Bring to the boil, cover and cook for 25 minutes or until the stock has been absorbed and the rice is tender. Finely slice half the mint leaves. Stir the spring onions, sliced mint, coriander leaves, chilli and chicken into the rice. Divide between four plates and top with a slice of tofu. Splash the tofu with some soy, and serve with a lime wedge and more mint leaves. Serves 4

pancetta and pea risotto

2 tablespoons butter
1 onion, finely diced
8 slices pancetta, finely diced
4 sage leaves
220 g (1 cup) arborio rice
1 litre (4 cups) hot chicken stock
150 g (1 cup) frozen peas
75 g ($^{3}/_{4}$ cup) grated Parmesan cheese
15 g ($^{1}/_{2}$ cup) roughly chopped parsley
10 mint leaves, finely chopped
extra virgin olive oil
grated Parmesan cheese

Heat the butter in a large saucepan over a medium heat, add the onion, pancetta and sage and sauté until the onions are soft and transparent. Add the rice and stir for a minute until it is well coated and glossy.

Add about 250 ml (1 cup) of stock and simmer, stirring until it is completely absorbed. Add more stock, and when the liquid has been absorbed, add the peas and more stock. Cook until all the liquid has been absorbed and then test the rice to see if it is *al dente*. If it needs further cooking, add a little more stock or water.

Fold in the Parmesan and work it into the risotto before adding the parsley and mint at the last minute. Serve with a drizzle of extra virgin olive oil and some more Parmesan. Serves 4

tomato and tofu broth

1 litre (4 cups) dashi stock (basics)
2 teaspoons mirin
4 tablespoons white miso paste
1 tablespoon grated fresh ginger
4 Roma (plum) tomatoes
300 g (10$^{1}/_{2}$ oz) silken firm tofu
120 g (4 handfuls) baby spinach leaves
1 tablespoon soy sauce

Put the dashi stock, mirin, white miso paste and ginger into a saucepan and bring to the boil, then reduce the heat to a gentle simmer.

Slice the tomatoes in half and scoop out the seeds using a spoon. Discard the seeds, dice the tomato flesh and add the tomatoes to the broth, simmering for a further 10 minutes.

Cut the tofu into cubes and put it into four soup bowls. Add the spinach leaves and soy sauce to the broth and cook for a minute until the leaves have just wilted. Ladle the soup over the tofu and serve immediately. Serves 4

fresh and fast

- The white chicken salad could be made with other ingredients. Try cooking the rice in a vegetable stock with a little fresh ginger. Add the fresh herbs and top with seared tuna and a sprinkle of sesame seeds.

- Instant miso soup is another great store cupboard secret, perfect for those nights when you have little time to spend over the stove but want something warm and comforting to eat. Cook a serve of Asian-style noodles or fine pasta and add them to a warmed bowl along with some instant miso. Top with sliced spring onions (scallions), tofu, pickled ginger, spinach leaves or whatever else comes to hand.

- Boil fresh peas until they are soft, then drain them and mash with some butter, grated fresh ginger and a little lemon juice. Season to taste and serve the peas topped with some pan-fried fish fillets.

winter vegetable chicken

Farm-fresh baby carrots need little more than a rinse and a trim. Add them whole to stews or simply toss them in a little butter as a side dish.

red mullet with tomato and fennel sauce

winter vegetable chicken

30 g (1/4 cup) plain (all-purpose) flour
2 teaspoons sea salt
1 teaspoon ground roast cumin seeds
2 chicken legs
2 chicken thighs
1 carrot, peeled and cut into small chunks
1 turnip, peeled and cut into small chunks
1 parsnip, peeled and cut into small chunks
1 white onion, sliced
2 celery stalks, trimmed and sliced
1 leek, washed and sliced
250 ml (1 cup) chicken stock or water
roughly chopped flat-leaf (Italian) parsley

Preheat the oven to 180°C (350°F/Gas 4). Put the flour and seasonings into a bowl and toss the chicken pieces so that they are well covered with the seasoned flour.

Put half the vegetables into the base of a casserole and then top with the chicken (shake off any excess seasoning). Add the remaining vegetables and stock, cover the dish with a lid or foil and put in the oven for 1 hour and 20 minutes. Remove the chicken and serve immediately with a scattering of freshly chopped parsley. Serves 2

red mullet with tomato and fennel sauce

2 teaspoons sea salt
2 teaspoons fennel seeds
20 mint leaves
1 tablespoon olive oil
4 ripe tomatoes, finely chopped
125 ml (1/2 cup) white wine
2 small fennel bulbs, finely sliced
4 x 175 g (6 oz) or 2 x 350 g (12 oz) red mullet,
   gutted and scaled
2 tablespoons extra virgin olive oil

Preheat the oven to 180°C (350°F/Gas 4). Put the sea salt, fennel seeds and mint leaves in a mortar and pestle or blender and grind them together. When the leaves and seeds have begun to break down, add the oil to make a thin paste.

Put half of the tomatoes, the wine and half the fennel into a casserole dish. Rinse the mullet in cold water and dry with paper towels, then rub with the fennel paste and put the fish on top of the tomatoes. Stuff some of the remaining fennel into the fish cavities and scatter the rest over the fish, along with the remaining tomatoes. Cover with a lid and bake for 25 minutes. To serve, carefully remove the whole fish and put them on warmed serving plates. Spoon the sauce over the fish, season with freshly ground black pepper and drizzle with a little olive oil. Serves 4

pappardelle with basil, feta and roast capsicum

4 red capsicums (peppers)
3 tablespoons extra virgin olive oil
1 teaspoon balsamic vinegar
120 g (1 bunch) basil
400 g (14 oz) pappardelle
150 g (51/2 oz) feta cheese

Preheat the oven to 200°C (400°F/Gas 6). Rub the capsicums with a little oil, slice them in half lengthways and put them on a baking tray with the skin facing up. Bake them for 20 minutes or until the skin blackens and blisters. Put the capsicums in a plastic bag or bowl covered in plastic wrap, allow them to cool and then remove the skin and seeds. Put the flesh of the capsicum into a blender with the balsamic vinegar and 10 basil leaves, season and blend. Add the strained liquid from the baking tray and a little olive oil to give the capsicums a sauce consistency, then put the sauce in a large saucepan over a low heat to keep it warm.

Cook the pappardelle until it is *al dente*, then drain the pasta and add it to the warm capsicum sauce. Crumble half the feta through the pasta and toss everything together. Serve garnished with basil leaves and the rest of the feta crumbled on top. Serves 4

roast chicken with an almond sauce

4 whole chicken legs (Marylands)
2 tablespoons olive oil
8 sprigs lemon thyme
625 ml (21/2 cups) chicken stock
100 g (1 cup) ground almonds
1 garlic clove, crushed
2 tablespoons finely chopped parsley
1/2 teaspoon sugar
1 lemon, juiced
1 pinch saffron
leaf salad

Preheat the oven to 200°C (400°F/Gas 6). Rub sea salt into the skin of the chicken legs before putting them onto a baking tray. Drizzle the Marylands with olive oil, cover with the thyme and then roast for 40 minutes or until the chicken is cooked through. Remove the chicken from the oven and allow it to rest for a minute before serving with the almond sauce.

To make the sauce, bring the stock and ground almonds to the boil in a saucepan. Reduce to a simmer, season to taste with sea salt and white pepper and then add the other ingredients. Simmer gently for a further 20 minutes before spooning the sauce over the roast chicken. Serve with a salad of mixed leaves. Serves 4.

warm salad of avocado and prosciutto

1 teaspoon thyme leaves
1/2 teaspoon brown sugar
1 teaspoon Dijon mustard
3 tablespoons extra virgin olive oil
1 tablespoon balsamic vinegar
2 avocados, thickly sliced
2 Lebanese (small) cucumbers, thinly sliced
2 tablespoons toasted pine nuts
120 g (4 handfuls) mesclun salad mix
6 slices prosciutto

To make the dressing, blend the thyme, brown sugar, mustard, oil and vinegar together in a small bowl. Arrange the avocados, cucumbers and pine nuts on top of the mesclun salad.

Slice the prosciutto into 4 cm (11/2 in) pieces and grill or fry until it is crisp and golden. Tip the hot prosciutto into the salad dressing and toss together before pouring it over the salad. Serves 4

seared tuna with olive butter and warm red salad

1 red capsicum (pepper)
4 ripe tomatoes, quartered
1 red onion, cut into eighths
2 tablespoons extra virgin olive oil
2 tablespoons butter, softened
6 black olives, pitted and finely chopped
2 tablespoons finely chopped flat-leaf (Italian) parsley
4 x 150 g (51/2 oz) tuna fillets

Preheat the oven to 180°C (350°F/Gas 4). Slice the capsicum into thick strips and put it on a baking tray. Add the tomatoes and red onion, drizzle with the olive oil and season with sea salt and freshly ground black pepper. Cover the vegetables with foil and bake for 30 minutes.

Combine the butter, chopped olives and parsley.

Sear the tuna fillets in a pan for 2–3 minutes on both sides. Serve with the warm red salad and a dollop of the olive butter. Serves 4

smoked tofu and sesame salad

smoked tofu and sesame salad

55 g (1/3 cup) white sesame seeds, toasted
1 teaspoon sugar
1 1/2 tablespoons soy sauce
1 teaspoon fresh ginger juice
1 teaspoon rice vinegar
400 g (14 oz) Chinese greens or broccolini, cut into pieces
200 g (7 oz) smoked tofu, cut into cubes
2 spring onions (scallions), finely sliced
sesame seeds

Put the toasted sesame seeds, sugar, soy sauce, ginger juice and vinegar into a blender with 80 ml (1/3 cup) of water. Blend until it forms a rough paste and then put it in a small bowl. Blanch the greens in boiling salted water for a minute or until they turn bright green and are tender.

Pile the cooked greens onto a serving platter with the tofu, gently pour the sesame dressing over the salad and garnish with the finely sliced spring onion and a few more sesame seeds.
Serves 4 as a side dish

spiced barramundi

12 whole macadamia nuts
1/4 white onion, finely diced
4 garlic cloves
2 red chillies, seeded and finely chopped
2 teaspoons finely grated fresh ginger
1 teaspoon ground turmeric
4 tablespoons tamarind water (basics)
1 teaspoon soy sauce
4 x 200 g (7 oz) barramundi fillets
125 ml (1/2 cup) coconut milk
steamed Asian greens

Preheat the oven to 200°C (400°F/Gas 6). Whiz the nuts, onion, garlic, chillies, ginger, turmeric, tamarind water and soy sauce to a paste in a blender or food processor. Rinse the barramundi fillets in cold water and pat dry with paper towels. Rub half the paste over the fish, put it on a baking tray and bake for 12 minutes.

Put the remaining half of the paste into a small saucepan and add the coconut milk. Stir over a medium heat. When the fish is cooked, serve with steamed Asian greens and some of the coconut sauce. Serves 4

onion soup

2 tablespoons butter
8 onions, peeled and finely sliced
2 garlic cloves
1 tablespoon finely chopped rosemary
1 litre (4 cups) chicken stock
30 g (1 cup) roughly chopped flat-leaf (Italian) parsley
70 g (3/4 cup) grated vintage Cheddar cheese

Melt the butter in a large saucepan over a medium heat and then add the onions, garlic and rosemary. Cover and allow the onions to slowly sauté, stirring them occasionally until they are soft and have almost dissolved. This will take about half an hour.

Add the chicken stock, season with sea salt and ground white pepper and continue to cook for a further half hour. To serve, divide the soup between four large soup bowls and sprinkle the parsley and cheese on top. Serve immediately. Serves 4

fresh and fast

• Add finely sliced smoked tofu to your favourite vegetable stir-fry for extra heartiness.

• Marinate firm tofu overnight in mirin, soy sauce, freshly grated ginger and a teaspoon of sesame oil. Serve it with steamed rice and steamed Chinese greens.

• Sauté 4 finely sliced onions in a little butter. Add a teaspoon of rosemary, a teaspoon of brown sugar and 2 finely chopped garlic cloves. Cover and cook until the onions are soft and transparent, then reduce over a low heat to a marmalade consistency and stir in a little mustard. Serve with grilled sausages and mashed potato.

celeriac purée

duck breast with cucumber

115 g (1/2 cup) brown sugar
3 teaspoons grated fresh ginger
1 orange, zest grated, juiced
4 duck breast fillets
2 teaspoons sesame oil
3 teaspoons sesame seeds
6 Lebanese (small) cucumbers, halved and sliced
    on the diagonal
80 g (1 bunch) garlic chives, cut into lengths
1 tablespoon soy sauce

Put the brown sugar, 2 teaspoons of grated ginger and the orange zest into a bowl and mix them together. With a sharp knife, make several diagonal cuts across the skin of the duck breast. Rub the sugar mixture into the surface of the skin and leave it in the fridge to marinate for several hours or overnight.

Preheat the oven to 180°C (350°F/Gas 4). Put the duck breasts on a baking tray and roast them for 10 to 12 minutes. Remove the duck, cover and keep warm. Heat the sesame oil in a wok and add the sesame seeds and remaining ginger. As soon as the seeds begin to brown, add the cucumber and chives. Toss for a minute, then add the soy, orange juice and duck juices.

Put the duck under a hot grill for a minute to crisp up the skin. Serve the breasts sliced over the cucumber with rice. Serves 4

slow-baked tuna with lime leaves

600 g (1 lb 5 oz) piece tuna fillet
15 kaffir lime leaves
2 tablespoons pink peppercorns
250–500 ml (1–2 cups) light olive oil
lime mayonnaise (basics)

Preheat the oven to 120°C (250°F/Gas 1/2). Trim the tuna fillet, removing any of the dark flesh, and if the fillet is particularly thick slice it in half lengthways. Put the tuna in a loaf tin or small casserole dish. Season with some sea salt and scatter over the lime leaves and peppercorns, pour over enough oil to cover the fillet and then seal the top with a lid or aluminium foil. Put the tuna into the oven and bake for 45 minutes.

Lift the tuna out of the oil and serve it in thick slices with steamed potatoes, lime mayonnaise and wedges of fresh lime. Serves 4

celeriac purée

1 kg (2 lb 4 oz) celeriac
2 potatoes
1 teaspoon lemon juice
2 garlic cloves
2 tablespoons butter
1/4 white onion, finely diced
125 ml (1/2 cup) thick (double/heavy) cream

Peel and cut the celeriac and potato into large chunks and put them in a saucepan of cold water with the lemon juice and the two garlic cloves. Bring to the boil and cook for 25 minutes or until the celeriac is soft and you can easily push a sharp knife into it.

Drain the vegetables and return them to the pan with the butter and onion. Mash them, slowly adding the cream until you have a creamy mass. Season to taste and serve immediately. Serves 4

fresh and fast

- Stir-fried cucumber adds a delicious flavour and texture to stir-fries. Toss with broccolini, sliced green capsicum (pepper), spring onions (scallions) and a sauce of sesame oil, soy sauce, ginger, sesame seeds and fresh lemon juice.

- Grate a whole celeriac into a pot of sautéed onions. Pour in enough vegetable stock to cover the celeriac and add some finely chopped flat-leaf (Italian) parsley. Simmer until the celeriac is soft and beginning to dissolve — you may need to add a little stock to bring it back to a soupy consistency. Season to taste and serve the soup with toasted walnut bread and either a dash of cream or some crumbled goat's cheese.

- If you prefer your tuna only just seared, marinate 1 cm (1/2 in) thick slices in a marinade of lemon juice, olive oil and finely sliced lime leaves. Sear the tuna on both sides and serve with steamed greens, a noodle salad or the lime mayonnaise and boiled potatoes.

slow-baked tuna with lime leaves

lamb shanks with parsnip, lemon and herbs

4 red onions, quartered
6 garlic cloves, finely sliced
4 sprigs thyme
4 lamb shanks (about 1.2 kg/2 lb 12 oz)
1 large parsnip, peeled
8 sage leaves
250 ml (1 cup) veal stock
1 tablespoon small capers
1 garlic clove, crushed
1 lemon, zested
20 g (1 cup) flat-leaf (Italian) parsley leaves

Preheat the oven to 200°C (400°F/Gas 6). Make a bed of the red onions, garlic and thyme in a deep casserole dish. Put the shanks on top, then arrange the parsnip and sage leaves over them and season well. Pour over the veal stock and cover with a lid or foil. Bake for 1 hour, then uncover and bake for a further 30 minutes or until the meat is pulling away from the bones.

To make the gremolata, put the capers, garlic, lemon zest and parsley leaves on a chopping board and chop them together finely with a sharp knife. Serve sprinkled over the lamb shanks. Serves 4

ocean trout with salsa verde

1 thick slice white bread, crusts removed
40 g (2 cups) flat-leaf (Italian) parsley leaves
4 anchovies
1 teaspoon small capers
10 mint leaves
1 tablespoon Indian lime pickle or preserved lemon
80 ml (1/3 cup) light olive oil
4 x 175 g (6 oz) ocean trout fillets
2 tablespoons oil
boiled potatoes

To make the salsa verde, soak the bread in a bowl of water and then squeeze out any excess water — it should be soft but not wet. Put it into a food processor or blender with the parsley leaves, anchovies, capers, mint leaves, lime pickle and light olive oil and blend to form a thick sauce.

Rinse the trout fillets in cold water and pat them dry with some paper towels. Heat the oil in a frying pan over a high heat and add the fillets skin-side-down. Press them into the pan, ensuring that the heat hits the entire surface of the fillet. Cook for 2 minutes or until the skin is crisp and then turn them over. Reduce the heat to medium and cook for a further 3 minutes.

Serve the seared trout with the salsa verde, boiled potatoes and a sprinkling of salt. Serves 4

steamed barramundi with warm greens

1 tablespoon ground roast cumin
1 teaspoon thyme leaves
1/2 teaspoon ground turmeric
1 teaspoon sea salt
4 x 200 g (7 oz) barramundi fillets
3 tablespoons butter
3 zucchini (courgettes), sliced on the diagonal
150 g (5 1/2 oz) sugar snap peas, trimmed
1 tablespoon lemon juice

Put a large saucepan of water on to boil for the steamer. Tip the cumin, thyme, turmeric, sea salt and some ground black pepper into a clean plastic bag. Rinse the barramundi fillets in cold water and pat them dry with paper towels, then add the fish fillets to the bag and shake the bag to coat the fish in the spices.

Melt the butter in a large frying pan over a medium heat, add the zucchini and sauté them until they are beginning to soften. Then add the sugar snaps and lemon juice and cover the pan for a few minutes, allowing the peas to steam to a bright green. Put the fish on a plate in a steamer basket and cook it over simmering water for 4 to 5 minutes. Serve the fish with the lemony greens. Serves 4

seared lamb on ginger lentils

2 tablespoons olive oil
1 red onion, finely diced
2 garlic cloves, crushed
3 tablespoons grated fresh ginger
1 teaspoon ground roast cumin
200 g (1 cup) red lentils
2 lamb backstraps or pieces of fillet (about 500 g/1 lb 2 oz), trimmed
1 orange, zested and juiced
coriander (cilantro) leaves, roughly chopped

Preheat the oven to 180°C (350°F/Gas 4). Heat the oil in a saucepan over a medium heat and tip in the diced onion and the garlic. Cook for a minute or two until the onion is beginning to soften, and then add the ginger, cumin and red lentils. Stir for a minute or two so that the lentils are glossy and well coated in the spices, and then pour in 625 ml (2 1/2 cups) of water. Simmer for half an hour or until the lentils are soft.

Sear the lamb on both sides, then roast in the oven for 5 minutes. Remove the lamb, season, cover it with foil and let it rest for a minute. Add the orange zest to the lentils with the juice and most of the coriander. Season with sea salt and white pepper to taste. Spoon the hot lentils into four pasta bowls and top with slices of lamb. Season to taste. Drizzle with the pan juices and a little extra virgin olive oil and sprinkle with some coriander leaves. Serves 4

beef fillet with horseradish and garlic butter

With its burnished brown skin and sweet floury centre, the chestnut is the very essence of winter.

cider-glazed pork loin

beef fillet with horseradish and garlic butter

1.5 kg (3 lb 5 oz) beef eye fillet
2 tablespoons freshly ground black pepper
3 garlic bulbs
2 tablespoons butter
2 teaspoons grated fresh horseradish or horseradish sauce
sautéed baby carrots
sautéed chestnuts

Trim the fillet and then rub the pepper into the surface. Put it on a tray and leave it in the fridge, uncovered, overnight.

Preheat the oven to 200°C (400°F/Gas 6). Put the garlic bulbs on a tray and cook them in the oven for half an hour. Remove the bulbs and allow them to cool until they can be handled, then slice them in half and squeeze out the soft garlic. Mash this into the butter and mix in the horseradish. Season to taste.

Put the fillet into a roasting tin and roast for 10 minutes. Remove the fillet and turn it over before returning it to the oven for a further 5 minutes.

Season the beef with salt, cover it with foil and rest it for 15 minutes. Drain any juices from the roasting tin, retaining them to pour over the meat later.

Return the fillet to the oven for a further 10 to 15 minutes, depending on how rare you like your beef. Serve in thick slices with the garlic butter, a drizzle of the pan juices and some sautéed baby carrots and chestnuts. Season with black pepper. Serves 6

cider-glazed pork loin

500 ml (2 cups) apple cider
60 ml (1/4 cup) honey
3 garlic cloves, peeled and finely chopped
3 star anise
1 cinnamon stick
1 large red chilli, split in half
2 bay leaves
1 kg (2 lb 4 oz) pork loin, skin cut off and reserved
3 green apples, peeled, cored and thickly sliced
1 tablespoon balsamic vinegar

Put the cider, honey, garlic cloves, star anise, cinnamon, chilli and bay leaves in a bowl. Cut deep slashes diagonally over the loin and add the pork to the marinade. Roll it around so it is well coated, then cover it and put it in the fridge to marinate overnight.

Heat the oven to 200°C (400°F/Gas 6). Transfer the pork to a roasting tin, cover with foil and roast for 40 minutes. To make the crackling, score the pork skin lightly with a very sharp knife and cut it into several strips. Put the strips in a roasting tin, brush them with water, sprinkle with salt and roast for 20 minutes or until the skin is golden brown and crackly. Drain off any fat.

While the meat is cooking, put the apples in a saucepan with 125 ml (1/2 cup) of the marinating liquid. Bring to the boil and then leave to simmer for 15 minutes or until the liquid has reduced. Add the balsamic vinegar and season.

Uncover the pork and baste it with the pan juices. Cook it for a further 20 minutes or until the juices run clear when you insert a skewer into the meat. Stand the pork for 10 minutes before carving. Serve with apple relish, crackling and the warm salad of chestnuts and Brussels sprouts on page 145. Serves 6

spiced red cabbage

2 tablespoons light olive oil
2 garlic cloves, crushed
1 teaspoon fennel seeds
1 tablespoon mustard seeds
500 g (1 lb 2 oz) red cabbage, finely sliced
125 ml (1/2 cup) red wine

Heat the oil in a deep frying pan over a medium heat and add the garlic, fennel seeds and mustard seeds. As the mustard seeds begin to pop, add the cabbage and sauté for a minute. Add the red wine, then cover and simmer over a low heat for half an hour. This would go well with the cider-glazed pork loin on page 193, or with any roast meat. Serves 4

spicy vegetables with couscous

1 red onion, cut into eighths
2 garlic cloves, finely sliced
1 cinnamon stick
2 cm (3/4 in) piece fresh ginger, peeled and quartered
1 teaspoon paprika
1 generous pinch saffron
1 x 400 g (14 oz) tin chopped tomatoes
2 red capsicums (peppers), seeded and cut into pieces
1 tablespoon brown sugar
400 g (1 cup) cooked chickpeas
60 ml (1/4 cup) oil
4 Japanese eggplants (aubergines), sliced in half lengthways
80 g (1 bunch) coriander (cilantro), roughly chopped
buttered couscous (basics)

Put the onion, garlic, spices and tomatoes into a large saucepan, pour in 250 ml (1 cup) of water and bring to the boil. Add the capsicum, sugar and chickpeas, season and simmer for half an hour. Meanwhile, heat the oil in a frying pan over a high heat and fry the eggplants until golden and slightly puffy. Drain them on paper towels.

Remove the cinnamon and ginger chunks from the tomato sauce and stir in the coriander. Serve the eggplant with the tomato and capsicum sauce and buttered couscous. Serves 4

sausage and bean stew

2 x 400 g (14 oz) tins cannellini beans, rinsed
5 ripe Roma (plum) tomatoes, roughly chopped
400 g (14 oz) tin chopped tomatoes
2 leeks, roughly chopped
8 garlic cloves, peeled
1 tablespoon thyme leaves
250 ml (1 cup) white wine
350 g (12 oz) good-quality spicy thick sausages
15 g (1/2 cup) roughly chopped parsley

Preheat the oven to 180°C (350°F/Gas 4). Put the beans, all the tomatoes, leeks, garlic, thyme and white wine into a casserole or ovenproof dish.

Prick the skins of the sausages with a fork and then sear them in a frying pan over a high heat until they are browned on all sides. Cut the sausages into bite-size pieces and put them into the casserole dish. Lightly stir everything together, then cover the dish with a lid or foil and put it into the oven for an hour.

Sprinkle with the parsley before serving with warm crusty bread. Serves 4

herbed chicken in paper on buttered risoni

8 large sage leaves
1 leek, finely sliced into 8 cm (3 in) lengths
4 chicken breast fillets
2 tablespoons butter
400 g (14 oz) risoni
1 lemon, zest grated
30 g (1 cup) roughly chopped flat-leaf (Italian) parsley leaves

Preheat the oven to 180°C (350°F/Gas 4). Lay four 20 cm (8 in) squares of baking paper along your kitchen bench and arrange a sage leaf topped with some leek at the centre of each. Put a chicken breast on top of the leek, then season and dab with a little butter. Top with more leeks and another sage leaf and then wrap up each of the parcels. Put them on a baking tray and bake for 25 minutes.

Meanwhile, cook the risoni in salted boiling water until it is *al dente*. Drain and return to the warm pan with the remaining butter, lemon zest and parsley leaves. Stir to combine.

To serve, pile the risoni onto four warmed plates and serve the chicken either in its wrapping or turned out. Allow the chicken juices to spill over the pasta. Serves 4

lemon ricotta cake

vanilla-poached apricots

lemon ricotta cake

125 g (1 cup) sultanas
250 ml (1 cup) very strong Earl Grey tea
6 eggs, separated
500 g (2 cups) firm ricotta cheese
125 ml (^{1}/$_2$ cup) thick (heavy/double) cream
125 g (^{1}/$_2$ cup) caster (superfine) sugar
3 lemons, zest grated
lemon and Cointreau syrup (basics)

Preheat the oven to 180°C (350°F/Gas 4). Line a 20 cm (8 in) springform tin with baking paper.

Put the sultanas into the Earl Grey tea and allow them to soak. Whip the egg whites until they form stiff peaks. Put the ricotta cheese, egg yolks, cream, sugar and grated lemon zest into a large bowl and blend everything together. Drain the sultanas and add them to the ricotta mix before carefully folding in the egg whites.

Pour the mixture into the springform tin and bake for 40 minutes, then put a layer of foil over the cake to stop it burning and bake for a further 15 minutes. Test that the cake is firm all the way through before allowing it to cool.

Serve with lemon and Cointreau syrup and lemon- or vanilla-flavoured ice cream. Serves 10

mini chocolate cakes

125 g (4^1/$_2$ oz) unsalted butter
100 g (3^1/$_2$ oz) dark chocolate
185 ml (^{3}/$_4$ cup) strong coffee
250 g (1 cup) sugar
1 egg
1 teaspoon vanilla extract
80 g (^{3}/$_4$ cup) plain (all-purpose) flour
1 teaspoon baking powder
30 g (^{1}/$_4$ cup) cocoa
chocolate icing (basics)

Preheat the oven to 180°C (350°F/Gas 4). Put the butter, chocolate and coffee in a saucepan over a low heat and leave it until the chocolate has melted. Add the sugar, stirring until it has dissolved, then pour the chocolate mixture into a mixing bowl. Whisk in the egg and vanilla before sifting in the dry ingredients. Stir everything together.

Spoon the mixture into 12 patty cake tins lined with cases and bake for 15 minutes. Allow the cakes to cool before removing them and icing them. Serve with whipped cream or vanilla bean ice cream. Makes 12

vanilla-poached apricots

200 g (7 oz) dried apricots
1 vanilla bean, split
^{1}/$_2$ teaspoon rosewater
1 tablespoon honey
40 g (^{1}/$_3$ cup) toasted slivered almonds
250 g (1 cup) plain yoghurt

Put the apricots in a saucepan with the split vanilla bean and 625 ml (2^1/$_2$ cups) of water. Bring to the boil, then cover and allow the fruit to simmer on a low heat for an hour.

Remove the vanilla bean and stir in the rosewater and the honey. Serve with the toasted almonds and yoghurt or a swirl of warm custard. Serves 6

fresh and fast

- To make simple apple turnovers, toss thin apple slices in a little sugar, cinnamon and lemon zest. Cut out 12 cm (4^1/$_2$ in) rounds of butter puff pastry and spoon a little of the mixture into the centre of each circle. Turn over half of each pastry circle to form a half moon shape, then seal the edges. Put the turnovers on a baking tray, sprinkle them with sugar and prick the surface of the pastry with a fork. Bake them until they are golden brown and serve hot.

- Finely slice 10 dried figs and cover them with hot water, the juice and zest of 1 orange, cinnamon and a teaspoon of rosewater. Allow the figs to sit overnight and serve them spooned over ice cream.

- Sometimes there is nothing finer than a slice of crisp green apple and a sliver of strong bitey Cheddar cheese. Serve with some freshly cracked walnuts or almonds.

winter fruit crumble

When it comes to rhubarb, the more wonderful the colour, the sweeter the flavour.

winter fruit crumble

300 g (1 bunch) rhubarb, roughly chopped
1 orange, juiced
6 dried figs, finely sliced
2 green apples, peeled and roughly chopped
60 g (1/4 cup) caster (superfine) sugar
60 g (1/2 cup) plain (all-purpose) flour
95 g (1/2 cup) brown sugar
95 g (1/2 cup) ground almonds
3 tablespoons unsalted butter

Preheat the oven to 180°C (350°F/Gas 4). Toss the rhubarb with the orange juice, figs, green apples and caster sugar and tip the mixture into an ovenproof dish.

Put the flour, brown sugar and ground almonds in a bowl, and then add the butter and rub it into the dry ingredients until the mixture begins to resemble breadcrumbs. Cover the fruit with this mixture and bake for 45 minutes. Serve with pouring cream or vanilla custard. Serves 6

baked apples

2 small panettone (about 100 g/3 1/2 oz each) or 1 large one
2 tablespoons brown sugar
4 large green apples
2 tablespoons unsalted butter
icing (powdered) sugar

Preheat the oven to 180°C (350°F/Gas 4). Line a baking tray with baking paper. Trim off the rounded top of one of the small panettone and slice the cake into four rounds, or cut four rounds from four slices of a large panettone. Place the rounds on the baking tray and lightly butter them.

Core the apples with an apple corer or a small sharp knife, making sure that you remove all the tough core pieces. Slice and butter the other small panettone, or some of the large one, before tearing it into small pieces. Stuff the small buttered panettone pieces into the centre of the apples, alternating the pieces with a little brown sugar.

Top with a teaspoon of brown sugar per apple and a dob of butter. Put the apples onto the four panettone rounds and bake them for 40 minutes.

Serve warm, dusted with icing sugar and accompanied with thick cream or vanilla custard. Serves 4

apple and pecan crumble cake

rhubarb syllabub

apple and pecan crumble cake

125 g (1 cup) plain (all-purpose) flour
2 teaspoons baking powder
370 g (2 cups) brown sugar
2 teaspoons cinnamon
125 g (4 1/2 oz) unsalted butter
125 ml (1/2 cup) milk
2 eggs
100 g (1 cup) pecan nuts, chopped
2 green apples, peeled and finely sliced
whipped cream or yoghurt

Preheat the oven to 180°C (350°F/Gas 4). Line a 20 cm (8 in) springform tin with baking paper. Combine the flour, baking powder, sugar and cinnamon in a food processor, then add butter and whiz until the mixture begins to resemble breadcrumbs. Put half of this mixture into the lined tin.

Add the milk and eggs to the processor with the remaining mixture and blend again to make a batter, then fold in the chopped pecans. Scatter the sliced apple over the crumble base and cover with the batter. Bake for an hour and test with a skewer to see if the cake is cooked through.

Allow the cake to cool before turning it out onto a serving plate. Serve slightly warm with whipped cream or yoghurt. Serves 10

pear and cardamom tart

185 g (1 3/4 cup) ground almonds
110 g (4 oz) unsalted butter
125 g (1/2 cup) caster (superfine) sugar
3 eggs
1/2 teaspoon ground cardamom
3 teaspoons cocoa
1 x 25 cm (10 in) prebaked shortcrust pastry case (basics)
2 ripe beurre bosc pears

Preheat the oven to 180°C (350°F/Gas 4). Put the ground almonds, butter, all the sugar except for 2 tablespoons, the eggs, cardamom and cocoa into a food processor and blend to form a thick paste. Carefully spoon and spread the mixture into the prebaked pastry case.

Quarter and core the pears, then slice them thickly, arranging the slices in a fan over the top of the almond mixture. Bake for 20 minutes.

Take the tart out of the oven and sprinkle the top with the rest of the sugar. Return it to the oven for a further 10 minutes and then test to check that the tart is cooked all the way through. Allow it to cool slightly before transferring it to a serving plate. Serves 8

rhubarb syllabub

500 g (1 lb 2 oz) rhubarb, cut into small pieces
90 g (1/3 cup) caster (superfine) sugar
250 ml (1 cup) thick (double/heavy) cream
16 macaroons or amaretti
4 tablespoons Madeira
1 teaspoon finely grated lemon zest
1/4 teaspoon almond extract

Put the rhubarb in a saucepan with the sugar, then cover and cook over a medium heat until the rhubarb is soft, stirring occasionally to prevent it from sticking. Leave it to cool. Whip the cream and put it into the fridge, covered, until you are ready to use it.

Crumble two macaroons into each of eight glasses. Fold the Madeira, lemon zest and almond extract into the rhubarb before lightly folding the rhubarb through the whipped cream. Spoon the rhubarb cream over the macaroons and serve. Serves 8

fresh and fast

- Take one sheet of frozen puff pastry and cut it in half to form two rectangles. Spread some apricot jam over one of the rectangles and then cover it with the remaining rectangle. Press the edges together. Put the pastry on a lined baking tray, top with thin slices of pear, brush with butter and then sprinkle with cinnamon sugar. Put it in the oven and bake until it is golden brown. Serve in slices with double cream.

- Serve stewed rhubarb with creamy Bircher muesli for a great winter breakfast, or pile it into bowls while it is still warm and serve with a dollop of yoghurt and some toasted shredded coconut

- Simmer finely chopped rhubarb with sugar over a low heat until it has reduced to a thick, sweet mass. Spoon the cooled rhubarb into the centre of individual pavlovas and top with cream and a drizzle of melted dark chocolate.

pear and cardamom tart

basics

lime mayonnaise

2 egg yolks
1 lime, zested and juiced
250 ml (1 cup) oil
sea salt

Whisk the egg yolks, lime zest and juice together in a large bowl. Slowly drizzle in the oil while whisking until the mixture thickens, and keep whisking the mixture until it becomes thick and creamy. Season to taste with the salt. If the mixture is very thick, add a little cold water until you achieve the right consistency.

roast sweet potato

2 large orange sweet potatoes (kumera)
1 tablespoon oil
sea salt

Preheat the oven to 180°C (350°F/Gas 4). Peel the sweet potatoes and cut them into chunks. Toss the potatoes in the oil and season with a good sprinkling of sea salt and some freshly ground black pepper.

Spread the potatoes out on a baking tray in a single layer and roast them for 30 minutes or until they are browned and cooked through. Serves 4

mashed potato

4 large floury potatoes, peeled
2 tablespoons milk
2 tablespoons butter

Cut the potatoes into pieces and cook them in simmering water for 15 minutes, or until they are soft. Drain them well, put them back in the pan with the milk and butter and then mash them until they are smooth. Season with salt and pepper. Serves 4

buttered couscous

200 g (1 cup) instant couscous
2 tablespoons butter

Bring 250 ml (1 cup) water to the boil in a saucepan and throw in the couscous. Take the pan off the heat, add the butter in small pieces and leave it to stand for 10 minutes.

Fluff the couscous up with a fork and season well with salt and black pepper. Serves 4

pesto

150 g (1 bunch) basil, leaves removed
140 g (1 bunch) flat-leaf (Italian) parsley, roughly chopped
100 g (1 cup) grated Parmesan cheese
1 garlic clove
80 g (1/2 cup) pine nuts, toasted
170 ml (2/3 cup) olive oil

Put the basil, parsley, Parmesan, garlic and pine nuts into a food processor or a pestle and mortar and blend or pound the mixture to make a thick paste.

Add the oil in a steady stream until the paste has a spoonable consistency.

If you want to keep your pesto, put it in a sterilized jar and add a layer of olive oil on top. This will prevent the surface of the pesto oxidizing and turning brown. Keep the pesto in the fridge for up to 2 weeks.

croutons

6 pieces thick-sliced white bread
125 ml (1/2 cup) oil

Remove the crusts from the bread and cut it into small cubes. Heat the oil in a frying pan, and when the surface of the oil has started to shimmer add the cubes of bread and reduce the heat. Toss the bread in the oil until the croutons are golden brown.

Remove the croutons with a slotted spoon and drain them on paper towels. Season with salt and pepper.

tomato sauce

6 Roma (plum) tomatoes
10 basil leaves
1 teaspoon sugar
1 garlic clove
2 tablespoons extra virgin olive oil
1 teaspoon balsamic vinegar

Preheat the oven to 200°C (400°F/Gas 6). Put the tomatoes on a baking tray and roast them in the oven until their skins are beginning to blacken on all sides.

Put the tomatoes into a food processor or blender with the basil leaves, sugar, garlic, olive oil and vinegar. Blend to form a thick sauce, thinning the mixture with a little warm water if necessary. This will keep for 2 to 3 days in the fridge.

rouille

1 thick slice sourdough bread
1 pinch saffron threads
1 red capsicum (pepper), roasted and skinned
1/4 teaspoon paprika
2 garlic cloves
125 ml (1/2 cup) light olive oil

Tear the bread into pieces and put it in a bowl. Bring the saffron threads and 60 ml (1/4 cup) of water to the boil in a small saucepan and simmer for a minute. Pour the hot saffron water over the bread.

Allow the bread to soak in the water and then add it to a food processor or blender with the capsicum, paprika and garlic. Blend to form a smooth paste, then add the olive oil in a stream to give a thick consistency. Season with salt to taste.

tapenade

75 g (1/2 cup) pitted black olives
1 garlic clove
15 g (1/2 cup) roughly chopped flat-leaf (Italian) parsley leaves
10 basil leaves
2 anchovy fillets
1 teaspoon capers
125 ml (1/2 cup) olive oil

Put all the ingredients except the oil in a blender or food processor and blend to a rough paste. Add the oil in a stream until you reach the desired consistency. Season with freshly ground black pepper to taste.

basic vinaigrette

2 tablespoons vinegar
125 ml (1/2 cup) olive oil
1 teaspoon Dijon mustard

Whisk all the ingredients together and season to taste. You may like to add other flavours, such as fresh thyme, basil or rosemary. The vinegar can be replaced with lemon juice.

dashi stock*

30 g (1 oz) dried kombu
20 g (3/4 oz) bonito flakes

Put 2 litres (8 cups) of cold water and the kombu in a saucepan and slowly bring it to the boil over a medium heat. Regulate the heat so that the water takes around 10 minutes to come to the boil. As it nears boiling point, test the thickest part of the seaweed: if it is soft to the touch and your thumbnail easily cuts into the surface, remove the kombu.

Let the water come back to the boil, then add half a glass of cold water and pour in the bonito flakes. As soon as the stock returns to the boil, remove it from the heat and skim the surface. When the bonito flakes have sunk to the bottom of the pan, strain the stock through a square of muslin or a very fine sieve. The finished stock should be clear and free of bonito flakes.

* Instant dashi is available in most large supermarkets, health food stores or specialty Asian shops.

tamarind water

100 g (31/2 oz) tamarind pulp

To make tamarind water, put the tamarind pulp in a bowl and cover it with 500 ml (2 cups) of boiling water. Allow it to steep for 1 hour, stirring occasionally to break up the fibres, then strain.

shortcrust tart case

200 g (1²/₃ cups) plain (all-purpose) flour
100 g (3¹/₂ oz) unsalted butter
1 tablespoon caster (superfine) sugar

Put the flour, butter, sugar and a pinch of salt into a food processor and process for 1 minute. Add 2 tablespoons of chilled water and pulse until the mixture comes together. Wrap the dough in plastic wrap and chill for 30 minutes.

Roll the pastry out as thinly as possible* and line a greased 25 cm (10 in) tart tin or six 8 cm (3 in) tartlet tins. Chill for a further 30 minutes. Prick the base, line it with crumpled greaseproof paper and fill with rice or baking weights. Place the tin in a preheated 180°C (350°F/Gas 4) oven for 10 to 15 minutes or until the pastry looks cooked and dry. Remove and allow to cool. Makes 1 tart case**

* The easiest way to do this is to roll it out between two layers of plastic wrap.

** Tart cases that are not used immediately can be stored in the freezer for several weeks. Put the tart case in a preheated oven direct from the freezer (there's no need to thaw the case first).

lemon and cointreau syrup

3 lemons, juiced
60 g (¹/₄ cup) sugar
1 star anise
2 tablespoons Cointreau

Put the lemon juice, sugar and star anise in a small saucepan. Bring to the boil, then reduce the heat, allowing the mixture to simmer for a few minutes. Remove from the heat and let it cool before adding Cointreau. This syrup will keep for a couple of weeks in the fridge.

cardamom almond bread

3 egg whites
80 g (¹/₃ cup) caster (superfine) sugar
85 g (²/₃ cup) plain (all-purpose) flour
2 oranges, zested
90 g (¹/₂ cup) blanched almonds
¹/₄ teaspoon ground cardamom

Preheat the oven to 180°C (350°F/Gas 4). To make the almond bread, oil an 8 x 22 cm (3 x 9 in) loaf tin and line it with baking paper. Whip the egg whites until they are stiff and then slowly whisk in the sugar. When the sugar has been fully incorporated and the whites are glossy, fold in the flour, orange zest, almonds and cardamom. Spoon the mixture into the prepared tin and bake it for 40 minutes.

Cool the almond bread on a wire rack. When it is cold, cut it into thin slices with a serrated knife and spread the slices out on a baking tray. Bake at 140°C (275°F/Gas 1) for 15 minutes or until the slices are crisp. Allow them to cool completely on a wire rack before storing them in an airtight container.

vanilla-glazed oranges

4 tablespoons caster (superfine) sugar
4 tablespoons orange juice
1 vanilla bean, split
4 oranges, segmented

Put the sugar, juice and vanilla bean in a saucepan and heat them gently together until the sugar dissolves. Turn up the heat and bubble the mixture until it begins to turn thick, sticky and toffee-like.

Add the orange segments and stir them gently into the mixture so that they are completely coated in toffee.

vanilla ice cream

8 egg yolks
200 g (7 oz) caster (superfine) sugar
375 ml (1¹/₂ cups) milk
375 ml (1¹/₂ cups) cream
1 vanilla bean, split

Whisk together the egg yolks and sugar until thick and creamy. Put the milk and cream in a saucepan with the split vanilla bean. Bring the milk just to the boil, then pour the hot milk into the sugar and egg mixture while still whisking.

Pour the custard back into the saucepan and continue to stir over a low heat* until the custard is thick enough to coat the back of a wooden spoon. Take out the vanilla bean and scrape the seeds into the mixture. Allow the ice cream mixture to cool.

Put the mixture into an ice cream maker and churn, following the manufacturer's instructions. Alternatively, put it in a freezer-proof box and freeze. Take the ice cream mixture out of the freezer every couple of hours and beat it. This will break up any ice crystals as they form and make the ice cream creamier.

* Don't boil the custard or it will split.

toffee apples

4 green apples, peeled, cored and cut
    into eighths
3 tablespoons caster (superfine) sugar
1 teaspoon cinnamon

Toss the apple pieces with the sugar,
cinnamon and 2 tablespoons of water.

Tip them into a heavy-based frying pan
over a medium heat and let them
caramelize and brown. Turn each of the
apple pieces as they begin to caramelize
and take them out when they are cooked
on both sides.

custard

2 egg yolks
2 tablespoons caster (superfine) sugar
310 ml (1 1/4) cups milk
1 vanilla bean, split

Whisk together the egg yolks and sugar
until thick and creamy. Put the milk in a
saucepan with the split vanilla bean. Bring
the milk just to the boil, then pour the hot
milk into the sugar and egg mixture while
still whisking.

Pour the custard back into the saucepan
and continue to stir over a low heat* until
the custard is thick enough to coat the
back of a wooden spoon. Take out the
vanilla bean and scrape the seeds into
the mixture.

* Don't boil the custard or it will split.

chocolate tart case

160 g (5 1/2 oz) unsalted butter
185 g (1 1/2 cups) plain (all-purpose) flour
2 tablespoons cocoa powder

Put all the ingredients in a food processor
and whiz to form a paste. If the pastry
doesn't ball together, add a dash of chilled
water. Cover the pastry in plastic wrap and
put it in the fridge for half an hour.

Roll the pastry out as thinly as possible*
and use it to line a 25 cm (10 in) tart tin.
Chill the pastry until it is ready to use.

To bake, preheat the oven to 180°C
(350°F/Gas 4). Cover the pastry with a
layer of crumpled baking paper weighted
down with baking weights, dried
beans or raw rice and put it in the oven
for 15 minutes.

Remove the paper and weights and bake
for a further 5 minutes or until the base of
the pastry is cooked through and looks
dry. Makes 1 tart case

* The easiest way to do this is to roll it out
between two layers of plastic wrap.

chocolate icing

100 g (3 1/2 oz) dark chocolate
125 ml (1/2 cup) thick (heavy/double)
    cream
1 tablespoon Frangelico
1 teaspoon ground cinnamon

To make the icing, put the chocolate and
cream into a small saucepan over a very
low heat. As the cream begins to get hot,
remove the pan from the heat and stir the
chocolate until it has melted into the
cream to form a thick sauce. Stir in the
liqueur and cinnamon and then set the
mixture aside to cool a little before icing
your cake.

cardamom and rosewater syrup

110 g (1/2 cup) sugar
1 teaspoon lemon juice
5 cardamom pods, lightly crushed
1/2 teaspoon rosewater

Put the sugar, lemon juice and cardamom
pods in a small saucepan and add 250 ml
(1 cup) of water. Bring slowly to the boil,
making sure that the sugar dissolves
completely, then reduce the heat and
simmer the mixture for 5 minutes.

Remove the syrup from the heat and stir in
the rosewater.

This syrup will keep for a couple of weeks
in the fridge.

pancake mix

125 g (1 cup) self-raising flour
1 teaspoon caster (superfine) sugar
1 egg
185 ml (2/3 cup) milk

Blend the flour, sugar, egg and a pinch of
salt together in a large bowl to form a thick
batter, then slowly whisk in the milk. Make
sure you remove any lumps as you whisk.
Cover the mixture and put it in the fridge
until you are ready to use it.

glossary

balsamic vinegar

Balsamic vinegar is a dark, fragrant, sweetish aged vinegar made from grape juice. The production of authentic balsamic vinegar is carefully controlled. Bottles of the real thing have 'Aceto Balsamico Tradizionale de Modena' written on the label, while commercial varieties simply have 'Aceto Balsamico de Modena'.

bamboo steamer

This inexpensive woven bamboo container has a lid and a slatted base. Food is put inside the container and then placed over a saucepan of boiling water to cook. Bamboo steamers are available from Asian grocery stores and most large supermarkets.

betel leaves

These are the aromatic, lacy-edged green leaves from the betel pepper. They can be found in Indian shops.

black sesame seeds

Mainly used in Asian cooking, black sesame seeds add colour, crunch and a distinct nuttiness to whatever dish they garnish. They can be found in most Asian grocery stores. Purchase the seeds regularly, as they can become rancid with age.

bocconcini

These are small balls of mozzarella, often sold sitting in their own whey. When fresh they are soft and springy to the touch and taste distinctly milky. They are available from most delicatessens.

brown miso

Brown miso (hatcho miso) is a fermented paste of soya beans, salt and either rice or barley. Miso is used extensively in Japanese cooking, in soups, dressings, stocks and as an ingredient in sauces and pickles. Brown miso has a richer flavour than white miso. It is available from Asian shops and health food stores.

butter puff pastry

This is puff pastry made with butter rather than vegetable fat, which gives it a much more buttery flavour than standard puff. If you can't find any, use ordinary puff pastry and brush it with melted butter to add flavour.

capers

Capers are the green buds from a Mediterranean shrub, preserved in brine or salt. Salted capers have a firmer texture and are often smaller than those preserved in brine. Rinse away the brine or salt before using them. Capers are available from good delicatessens.

Chinese black beans

These salted black beans can be found either vacuum-packed or in tins in Asian food stores.

coconut cream

Slightly thicker than coconut milk, coconut cream is available in tins. If you can't get hold of it, use the thick cream off the top of a couple of tins of coconut milk instead. Pour the milk into a jug and leave it to settle — the cream will separate out at the top.

cream

Cream comes with differing fat contents. If it needs to be whipped it must have a fat content higher than 35 per cent. Single and light cream do not whip.

crème de framboise

A raspberry liqueur.

crème fraîche

A naturally soured cream which is lighter than sour cream, it is available at gourmet food stores and some large supermarkets.

curry leaves

These are the smallish green aromatic leaves of a tree native to India and Sri Lanka. Curry leaves give a distinctive flavour to south Indian dishes. They are usually either fried and added to the dish or used as a garnish at the end.

daikon

Daikon, or mooli, is a large white radish. Its flavour varies from mild to quite spicy, depending on the season and variety. Daikon contains an enzyme that aids digestion. It can be freshly grated or slow-cooked in broths, and is available from most large supermarkets or Asian grocery stores. Select firm and shiny vegetables with unscarred skins.

dashi granules

These can be made into instant dashi stock simply by adding boiling water.

dried porcini mushrooms

Dried porcini (cep) mushrooms can be found either in small packets or sold loose from a jar in delicatessens.

enoki mushrooms

These pale, delicate mushrooms have a long thin stalk and tiny caps. They are very fragile and need only a minimal cooking time.

feta cheese

Feta is a white cheese made from sheep's milk or goat's milk. The fresh cheese is salted and cut into blocks before being matured in its own whey. It must be kept in the whey or in oil during storage or it will deteriorate quickly. Persian feta is particularly creamy in style. Feta is available from delicatessens and most supermarkets.

fish sauce

This is a highly flavoured, salty liquid made from fermented fish, which is widely used in South Asian cuisine to give a salty, savoury flavour. Buy a small bottle and keep it in the fridge.

Frangelico

A hazelnut-flavoured Italian liqueur sold in a brown bottle shaped like a monk's robe.

fresh horseradish

Fresh horseradish is a large white root with a knobbly brown skin. It is very pungent with a spicy, hot flavour.

ginger juice

Fresh ginger juice is produced by finely grating fresh ginger and then squeezing the liquid from the grated flesh.

goat's curd

This is a soft, fresh cheese made from goat's milk, which has a slightly acidic but mild and creamy flavour.

haloumi cheese

Haloumi is a semi-firm sheep's milk cheese. It has a rubbery texture which becomes soft and chewy when the cheese is grilled or fried. It is available from delicatessens and most large supermarkets.

hijiki

Hijiki is a dried, roughly shredded brown seaweed that needs to be soaked before it is used. It is available from Japanese shops and some supermarkets.

Indian lime pickle

Lime pickle is available from Indian grocery stores or large supermarkets. It is usually served as a side dish in Indian cooking.

mascarpone cheese

This heavy, Italian-style set cream is used as a base in many sweet and savoury dishes. It is available from good delicatessens and supermarkets.

mesclun

Mesclun is a green salad mix originating in Provence, in France. This salad often contains a selection of young, small leaves.

mirin

Mirin is a rice wine used in Japanese cooking. It adds sweetness to many sauces and dressings, and is used for marinating and glazing dishes like teriyaki. It is available from Asian grocery stores and most large supermarkets.

mozzarella

Fresh mozzarella can be found in most delicatessens and is easily identified by its smooth, white appearance and ball-like shape. It is not to be confused with mass-produced mozzarella, which is mostly used as a pizza topping. Mozzarella is usually sold packed in whey.

mustard seeds

Mustard seeds have a sharp, hot flavour that is tempered by cooking. Both brown and yellow are available, although brown mustard seeds are more common.

natural ground almonds

These are ground almonds with their skins left on so that the meal is darker than ordinary ground almonds. They can be found in health food shops. Ground almonds can be used instead.

nori

Nori is an edible seaweed sold in paper-thin sheets. To concentrate the flavour, lightly roast the shiny side of the sheets over a low flame. Nori sheets are available from most large supermarkets, health food shops and Asian grocery stores.

orange flower water

This perfumed distillation of bitter-orange blossoms is mostly used as a flavouring in baked goods and drinks. It is available from delicatessens and large supermarkets.

oyster mushrooms

These beautifully shaped, delicately flavoured mushrooms are commonly greyish brown in colour but are also available in pink and yellow varieties.

palm sugar

Palm sugar is obtained from the sap of various palm trees and is sold in hard cakes or cylinders and in plastic jars. If it is very hard it will need to be grated. It can be found in Asian grocery stores or large supermarkets. Substitute dark brown sugar when palm sugar is unavailable.

pancetta

Pancetta is salted belly of pork. It is sold in good delicatessens, especially Italian ones, and some supermarkets. Pancetta is available either rolled and finely sliced or in large pieces ready to be diced or roughly cut. It adds a rich bacon flavour to dishes.

panettone

An aromatic northern Italian yeast bread made with raisins and candied peel, panettone is traditionally eaten at Christmas, when it is found in most Italian delicatessens or large supermarkets. Tiny ones are also available.

Persian feta cheese

see feta cheese

pesto

Available ready-made in most supermarkets, pesto is a puréed sauce traditionally made from basil, garlic, Parmesan cheese, pine nuts and olive oil.

pickled ginger

Japanese pickled ginger is available from most large supermarkets. The thin slivers of young ginger root are pickled in sweet vinegar and turn a distinctive salmon-pink colour in the process. (Bright pink ginger has been dyed.) The vinegar is an ideal additive to sauces where a sweet, gingery bite is called for.

pine mushrooms

Also known as matsutake, these Japanese mushrooms are brown in colour and thick and meaty in texture. They are best if cooked simply.

pink peppercorns

These are not true peppercorns but rather are the aromatic dried red berries from the tree *Schinus molle*.

plain yoghurt

Where recipes call for plain yoghurt use a good, thick variety like Greek or Greek-style. If the yoghurt seems watery, drain it in a muslin-lined sieve for about 2 hours.

pomegranate molasses

This is a thick syrup made from the reduction of pomegranate juice. It has a bittersweet flavour, which adds a sour bite to many Middle Eastern dishes. It is available from Middle Eastern specialty stores. The closest substitute is sweetened tamarind.

preserved lemon

These are whole lemons preserved in salt or brine, which turns their rind soft and pliable. Just the rind is used — the pulp should be scraped out and thrown away. It is available from delicatessens.

prosciutto

Prosciutto is lightly salted, air-dried ham. It is most commonly bought in paper-thin slices, and is available from delicatessens and large supermarkets. Parma ham and San Daniele are both types of prosciutto.

rice wine vinegar

Made from fermented rice, this vinegar comes in clear, red and black versions. Where just rice wine vinegar is called for, use the clear version.

ricotta cheese

Ricotta cheese can be bought cut from a wheel or in tubs. The wheel tends to be firmer in consistency and is better for baking. If you can only get ricotta in tubs, drain off any excess moisture by letting it sit for a couple of hours in a muslin-lined sieve.

risoni

Risoni are small rice-shaped pasta.

risotto rice

There are three well-known varieties of risotto rice that are widely available today: arborio, a large plump grain that makes a stickier risotto; vialone nano, a shorter grain that gives a loose consistency but keeps more of a bite in the middle; and carnaroli, similar in size to vialone nano, which makes a risotto with a firm consistency. All are interchangeable, although cooking times may vary by 5 minutes or so.

rosewater

The distilled essence of rose petals, rosewater is used to impart a perfumed flavour to pastries and sweet puddings. It is available from delicatessens and large supermarkets.

saffron threads

These are the orange-red stigmas of a type of crocus. Saffron is expensive and should be bought in small quantities. Use it sparingly as it has a very strong flavour.

sambal oelek

A hot paste made from pounded chillies, salt and vinegar, it is available from Asian grocery stores and most large supermarkets.

sashimi salmon

Salmon sold for making sushi and sashimi, which is intended to be eaten raw, is usually the freshest fish at the market. Buy a thick piece cut from the centre rather than a narrower tail end.

sesame oil

Sesame oil is available in two varieties. The darker, more pungent, type is made with roasted sesame seeds and comes from China, while a paler, non-roasted variety is Middle Eastern in origin.

shiitake mushrooms

These Asian mushrooms have white gills and a brown cap. Meaty in texture, they keep their shape very well when cooked. Dried shiitake are often sold as dried Chinese mushrooms.

Sichuan pepper

This is made from the dried red berries of the prickly ash tree, which is native to Sichuan in China. The flavour given off by the berries is spicy-hot and leaves a numbing aftertaste which can linger for some time. Dry-fry and crush the berries for the best flavour. Japanese sancho pepper is a close relative of Sichuan pepper and may be used instead.

smoked rainbow trout

Smoked rainbow trout is sold either as a whole fish or vacuum-packed as fillets. It can be hot- or cold-smoked. Remember to remove any small bones before using it.

somen noodles

These thin, wheat-based Japanese noodles are commonly sold dried and in bundles. They are available from Japanese specialty stores, Asian supermarkets and health food stores.

star anise

This is a pretty, star-shaped dried fruit that contains small, oval, brown seeds. Star anise has a flavour similar to that of anise but is more liquorice-like. It is commonly used whole because of its decorative shape.

sumac

Sumac is a peppery, sour spice made from dried and ground sumac berries. The fruit of a shrub found in the northern hemisphere, it is typically used in Middle Eastern cookery. It is available from most large supermarkets and Middle Eastern specialty stores.

tahini

This is a creamy paste made from ground sesame seeds. It is available in jars from most supermarkets.

tamarind

Tamarind is the sour pulp of an Asian fruit. It is most commonly available compressed into cakes or refined as tamarind concentrate in jars. Tamarind concentrate is widely available; the pulp can be found in Asian food shops. To make tamarind water from compressed tamarind, put 100 g (3 1/2 oz) of tamarind into a bowl and cover with 500 ml (2 cups) of boiling water. Allow to steep for 1 hour, stirring occasionally to break up the fibres, then strain. Use the concentrate according to the package instructions.

tortillas

This thin, round, unleavened bread is used in Mexican cooking as a wrap. Tortillas are available prepackaged in the refrigerator section of most supermarkets.

umeboshi plums

These are actually Japanese apricots coloured red and pickled in salt. They have a tangy, salty flavour. Umeboshi plums are available from health food shops and Japanese specialty shops.

vine leaves

The large, green leaves of the grapevine are available packed in tins, jars or plastic packs or in brine. They are used in Greek and Middle Eastern cookery to wrap foods for cooking. Vine leaves in brine should be rinsed before use to remove some of the salty flavour. Fresh, young vine leaves can be simmered in water for 10 minutes or until soft.

white miso

White miso (actually a pale yellow colour) is the fermented paste of soya beans, salt and either rice or barley. Miso is used extensively in Japanese cooking, in soups, dressings, stocks and as an ingredient in sauces and pickles. White miso has a sweet, mellow taste and a relatively low salt content. It is available from Asian grocery stores and health food stores.

witlof

Also called Belgian endive or chicory, this salad leaf has a bitter flavour and crisp, crunchy texture when raw. You can find witlof in both pale yellow and purple varieties.

wonton wrappers

These paper-thin sheets of dough are available either fresh or frozen from Asian grocery stores. They may be wrapped around fillings and steamed, deep-fried or used in broths. The wrappers come shaped both as squares and circles and are available in various thicknesses.

bibliography

Alexander, Stephanie. *The Cooks Companion*. Penguin Books, 1996.

Colwin, Laurie. *Home Cooking*. HarperCollins, 1988.

David, Elizabeth. *Summer Cooking*. Penguin Books, 1955.

Grigson, Sophie and Black, William. *Fish*. Headline Book Publishing, 2000.

Roden, Claudia. *Mediterranean Cookery*. BBC Books, 1987.

Solomon, Charmaine. *Encyclopedia of Asian Food*. New Holland Publishers, 2000.

Sreedharan, Das. *Fresh Flavours of India*. Conran Octopus, 1999.

Trang, Corinne. *Authentic Vietnamese Cooking*. Headline Book Publishing, 1999.

index